CONSIDERING
Jesus

Other Books by Joseph A. Tetlow, SJ

Making Choices in Christ

Always Discerning

You Have Called Me by My Name

CONSIDERING
Jesus

THE HUMAN EXPERIENCE OF THE REDEEMER

JOSEPH A. TETLOW, SJ

LOYOLAPRESS.
A JESUIT MINISTRY

Chicago

LOYOLA PRESS.
A JESUIT MINISTRY

www.loyolapress.com

Scripture citations, unless marked otherwise, are taken from the *New Revised Standard Version Anglicized Catholic Edition* (NRSVACE), copyright 1989, 1993, 1995, the Division of Christian Education of the National Council of Churches of Christ in the United States of America. All rights reserved. Used by permission.

Those so marked are from *The New Jerusalem Bible* (NJB), copyright 1985 by Darnton, Longman & Todd, Ltd. And Doubleday, a division of Bantam Doubleday Dell Publishing Group, Inc. Used with permission.

Cover art credit: Bernardo Ramonfaur/Shutterstock.com

ISBN: 978-0-8294-5527-4
Library of Congress Control Number: 2022948840

Printed in the United States of America.
22 23 24 25 26 27 28 29 30 31 Versa 10 9 8 7 6 5 4 3 2 1

Contents

Why Should We "Consider" Jesus? The Mandate He Gave Us

This book follows Jesus of Nazareth from His boyhood to His last days and Resurrection. It considers His experiences in several significant events as He *grew in wisdom, age, and grace* and as He did *the works* the *Father gave him to do.*[1]

The purpose of the book is to help disciples of Christ prayerfully obey Jesus' command: *Learn of me, for I am meek and humble of heart.*[2] It is true that Jesus reveals something profound about Himself here, but He does not mean to focus on Himself. He is focused on His disciples, giving them one of *my commandments.* All His life, Jesus was aware that He was and is *the way, the truth, and the life*, and He felt that He lived out that challenge successfully. For late in His life, He will say emphatically: *I have given you a model; that as I have done, you must also do.*[3]

His disciples understood Him well. Promptly after He left them, those who had known him began gathering the experiences that filled Jesus' public life and put them in gospel form. These Gospels are first the Good News that He brought from the Father. But in reporting His experiences of proclaiming that News, they also reveal a lot about Jesus' human character and spirituality. These Gospels are a living Word, for the Spirit was active in their gathering and the Spirit continues to be active in confirming their truth, "so that by hearing the message of salvation the whole world may believe, by believing it may hope, and by hoping it may love."[4]

About the Gospels' authenticity and veracity, we no longer have any reason—if Christians ever had—to doubt. We are blessed to have the rich resources of an immense body of scripture scholarship. Scholars have shown that the Gospels tell us a good deal about Jesus' own experiences. What did the young Jesus want when He stayed in the Temple? What drove him to *go to the other towns* in Galilee and Judea, and to heal on the Sabbath? What was Jesus doing in the Decapolis, preaching and healing a crowd of four thousand gentile pagans who listened to him for three days? What did He want to do for Simon the Pharisee? He discerned those *whom You gave me*, and He decided that He wanted Twelve as His close collaborators (why twelve?).

We now have credible answers to these questions, as Christian and Jewish scholars have placed Jesus in His religious, sociological, anthropological, and historical context. They have made study of the Gospels rich and rewarding.

They have also made this clear: we know a great deal about the life of our Redeemer. We can ask how He thought about things, what He perceived in the people around Him, and what happened when He spoke in the synagogues. These are the human experiences of the Son of Man, as He called Himself. But we are given the grace to know that this Person was and remains *the Christ, the Son of God*.[5] We believe what He said: *The Father and I are one*.[6] We do not believe in Jesus of Nazareth, who lived and died many years ago, any more than we believe in Muhammad or Joan of Arc. We *know* about Jesus, as we know about Muhammad and Joan, from adequate historical evidence. We believe in *Jesus Christ*, the Anointed One who rose from the dead to live forever in our flesh, and who now reigns as King of endless glory. Jesus Christ is the one we believe in.

Consequently, when we consider Jesus' human experience, we do it reverently and humbly. And at first, it might seem wrongheaded to ask what Jesus thought and felt. It can seem presumptuous and irreverent. But we must accept humbly that Jesus commanded us to do it. *Learn of me*, could not be clearer, and His emphatic declaration: *I have given you a model.*[7]

We have learned from the earliest disciples, who responded to Jesus' command practically and seriously. As the Gospel of Matthew was being finally edited,[8] Paul of Tarsus taught the Colossians that Jesus Christ *is the image of the unseen God.*[9] He was telling them that they do not need icons and idols; they have the living image. And before the Gospel of John had been finished, one of John's school and community wrote: *Whoever claims to abide in him ought to live as he lived.*[10] By that time, the synoptic Gospels were in circulation, and Christians had the *model and pattern* to show them how *to live as he lived*.

It is our turn now. For Paul explained to the Romans: God *had decided beforehand who were the ones destined to be molded to the pattern of his Son.*[11] That includes us. We have good reason—our Baptism, Confirmation, many Holy Communions—to think that we are among those so destined. It turns out that when we ponder and interpret Jesus' human experience, we—who are *being molded to the pattern of his Son*—can hardly avoid pondering and interpreting our own experience. The mature disciples of Christ do this in prayer.

This, then, is a book of, about, and for prayer. The purpose of this prayer is to consider the human experience of the Redeemer, as he invited and commanded us to do, and then to take it as *an example, a model*, so that we can *live as he lived* even many centuries after His life was finished.

Doing this requires a simple way of considering and contemplating events in Jesus' life. It means asking how He saw things such as keeping the Sabbath and how He appreciated people such as Peter and the widow of Nain. We are not applying a sophisticated academic method of inquiry but engaging a simple approach in prayer. As we ponder Jesus' human experiences, we want to beg "to know him more clearly, love him dearly, and follow him more nearly" (St. Richard of Chichester).

How Can We Consider Jesus' Experience? A Simple Yet Powerful Method

Christians have been on "the search for Jesus," applying modern methods of scholarship, for a century and a half. Yet, we do not find many books that explore the Redeemer's *actual human experiences*.

There are good reasons for this. During these years, scripture scholars have had to establish the most reliable texts of the gospels, their sources, and how they are related. They have had to clarify how the evangelists managed the information they had and what each writer's purposes were. In their work, they have placed Jesus in His historical context with truly remarkable thoroughness and accuracy.[12]

But these scholarly approaches deliberately put faith aside, determined to establish the "facts" as clearly and firmly as possible. Their methodologies have been hard to escape; it is hard to turn from reported fact to the process of experience. And as theologians have begun using other scholars' works, they had to keep our beliefs clear. So when Elizabeth Johnson wrote *Consider Jesus* (1993), it promised to be a book about His experience. But the book's subtitle, *Waves of Renewal in Christology*, indicate what the book achieved. It is rather about Jesus' theological significance than about His human experience.[13]

Luke Timothy Johnson's *The Real Jesus* (1997) pointed out how we can use and not be trammeled by the scholarship. He called for a new approach to the gospels: "an 'experience/interpretation' model." He pointed out what "the mature disciple of Christ" wants of this scholarship: "that it allows us to appreciate and appropriate the human experience of the Redeemer."[14]

Johnson's *The Real Jesus* called for a study like Gerhard Lohfink's *Jesus of Nazareth: What He Wanted, Who He Was* (2012). Lohfink tries to follow an "experience/interpretation" model, and in some good measure, achieves it, though his emphasis is on interpretation and framing Jesus' experiences in the purposes of the evangelists.[15]

With these and other studies reassuring us, we can now look directly at Jesus' human experiences *as experiences*. But how do we do this? We are so accustomed to reading these Gospel accounts and automatically going to the doctrines and "lessons" attached to them over years of Scripture readings, homilies, and so forth. It is our custom to skip over the actual experience of Jesus. To really see it, we need a simple method to help us slow down and *consider*.

The key is *enactment*. When people are involved in an event, they are not just "doing" something. A car or a computer just "does" things, according to its purpose and design. But when we as persons do something, we are *enacting* a whole complex of experiences. To begin with, we act unavoidably within a given context (situation, custom, community), and our experience is naturally subjective. When we "do" something, we are engaging our perspectives, our perceptions, our values, our desires, and our decisions.

If we take seriously that Jesus became one of us—was incarnated—then we realize that he, too, engaged in His experience in all these ways as well.

Thus, when we consider Jesus in the Gospels, we explore His experiences through these various facets.

But we don't stop there. Because *in him we live and move and have our being*, we want our own perspectives, perceptions, values, desires, and decisions to follow the model he has given us.[16] To summarize:

When we truly consider the experiences of Jesus, we can better learn how to follow His example.

In writing about the experiences along the arc of Jesus' life, I have carefully considered the following elements.

1. the current public context of the event
2. Jesus' condition, acts, behaviors, and habits
3. His perspective
4. His perception of things seen and felt
5. the values operating in Jesus, in His context
6. the desires that compelled Jesus
7. and the decisions Jesus made

These are all enacted in Jesus' experience and so contribute to an ongoing story—in Jesus' case, the history of the People. We might understand this best by applying it to one of Jesus' human experiences.

An Example of Considering:
Jesus Calls Zacchaeus in Luke 19

Context: Jesus and His disciples are walking to Jerusalem. They pass through Jericho, a wealthy city in a fertile region. It is a border town, so taxes and customs are high. Zacchaeus is one of the biggest tax collectors and *a wealthy man.*[17] As usual, Jesus is surrounded by a crowd.

Condition: Jesus faces almost twenty uphill miles to Jerusalem, and it seems to be getting on toward the day's main meal. He's hungry and he's on fire to spread the Good News of God's mercy. Jesus is familiar with who Zacchaeus is—everyone knows *that sinner.* Jesus also knows that among an oppressed people, tax collectors are despised.

Perspective: Jesus has always been ready to respond to anyone who approached him. In His view, Zacchaeus's running to climb up a tree is about the man's budding faith: he's opening himself to the Good News. Jesus also views His own fame as social permission to invite himself to a rich man's house. His culture's view is that he can invite himself and be welcomed.

Perception: Jesus will explain that he sees that Zacchaeus was, indeed, among *the lost* but not beyond repentance.[18] Jesus interprets Zacchaeus's keen desire to "see" him as a first step in friendship and perhaps an incipient repentance.

Then he sees the short man standing on one of the low branches of a sycamore tree. And in the man's quick response, Jesus perceives generosity: *if I have defrauded anyone of anything, I will pay back four times as much.* This is what Roman law imposed. The Jewish law required a fourfold return in only a few special cases, which did not include Zacchaeus's case.[19] So Jesus sees Zacchaeus's *"four times as much"* as the act of a generous spirit.

Value: Jesus values Zacchaeus as a *son of Abraham,* belonging to the People to whom he is sent. He rejects excluding him from God's forgiveness, as the upright thinkers did. Jesus knows from His own experience the rewards of generosity, and Zacchaeus's gift to the poor *of half of all I have* moves His heart.

Desire: Jesus wants Zacchaeus to accept the Good News. He also wants supper for this evening for himself and His disciples—and he is implicitly inviting the tax collector to repent. Also, *having nowhere to lay his head,* he is thinking of a place to stay overnight—*for I must stay at your house today.* Jesus wants Zacchaeus to accept the whole of His Good News and surely wants to *talk to him about the kingdom.* He loves the Zacchaeus he knows and wants to be loved by him. Jesus has a purpose: *the Son of Man came to seek out and to save the lost.*

Decision: Jesus decides to invite himself to dinner. *Zacchaeus, hurry and come down; for I must stay at your house today.* After Zacchaeus proclaims his generous restitutions, Jesus completes His experience with His new disciple, who he decides shows the Spirit's action: *Today salvation has come to this house, because he too is a son of Abraham.*

Enactment: Jesus is welcoming Zacchaeus into the kingdom. And that enactment is like a summary of the human experience of the Son among humankind.

We find that when we pray this way, looking through these various facets of experience, we are watching Jesus love His friends as he creates a community of faith and hope. This is the human experience of Jesus that we need to imitate today when individualism has poisoned the church and fractured the family. We really need Jesus' *example*, the *model I have given you.* We must follow it if we are ever to know how to *love one another as he has loved us.*

How to Use This Book

Each chapter has two parts: the first is *Context and Condition*, and the second, *Consider*.

The *Context and Condition* reminds us of the People's history in the first century and emphasizes the People's religious life and mind. It points out what can be said about Jesus' own situation as he experiences this event. The paragraphs make some points about how His culture and its customs shaped his experience. Sometimes they remind us of our own context and condition.

The *Consider* applies the seven elements, or facets, by which to look at an event in Jesus' life. In some passages, these seven elements are more evident and distinct, but as the chapters progress, the distinction among the seven elements becomes less evident though they are still operative. Note, too, that Jesus did not need to follow the order of the elements used here. For instance, His desire or decision might turn up in the first sentence of the Gospel account.

Each chapter ends with two thoughts *For Consideration*. The first suggests something to consider about Jesus' experience. The second, something to encourage prayer and reflection on our own experience.

The scriptures. Each chapter title includes the location of its event in a Gospel. Citations from the Gospels are in *italics*. Most have a footnote number; those without one are extensions of the former citation. They are, for the most part, exact citations of one of the current translations. Most are from the New Revised Standard Version Anglicized Catholic Edition, some from the Revised Standard Version, and some from the New Jerusalem Bible. The citations are from the four Gospels. I cite the other parts of the New Testament only in reference to our own experience of God in Christ.

I cite sources other than the Gospels only when I directly quote a clause or phrase that cannot be bettered or an idea or opinion that needs attribution. These are the authors gathered in the bibliography.

PART ONE

THE REDEEMER'S LONG HUMAN BEGINNING

1

How Things Are the Way They Are
John 1

Context and Condition

Before we begin to look at the human experience of the Redeemer, we'll do well to reflect a bit on our own current experience as His disciples.

First, it makes sense to point out that we have discovered more about the cosmos and the human race in recent decades than was discovered in all prior time together. Perhaps most radically, we learned that the beginning of all things is not so much mystery as fact demonstrated by science: the Big Bang. A Belgian priest, Monsignor Georges Lemaître, proved mathematically that time had a beginning. He imagined a "cosmic egg" that exploded and started the evolution that has brought us to where we are now.[20]

This has allowed Christians the new insight that God remains our Creator. He is *always* creating, sharing, being, moment by moment. The *Catechism* teaches it: God is creating the entire universe and everything in it "in a state of journeying."[21] Each one of us is entangled in this, whether we are aware of it or not. Almighty God is *always* creating each of us. We are not iron rods that God visits as occasional spurts of electricity; we are iron rods that are radioactive, and God is that radioactivity.

⌒∞⌒

The experienced disciple of Christ can correctly sense that God is *always* our Creator and Lord, always *creating* us and everything. This is our God, whom we find "in all things." St. Paul imagined us like mirrors facing the glory of the sun. A mirror can be full of light, a brilliant light—though it can produce none by itself. The mirror's light is the sun's light, shared. We're like that: full of light, our own light—yet it is His light—the light of the Son of Man.[22] For this is the way he understood himself in His maturity: *As the Father has life in Himself, so He has given to the Son to have life in Himself.*[23]

We need to grasp what that means to us: it's as though the sun were to come into earth and make the earth a ball of sunlight. Because that's what happened to humankind: the Son of God has come into the earth and made our flesh the source of eternal life. God gives each of us life, and each of us is to *give glory to God* by reflecting that life back to him, and as we do that, to one another.

How we are to give glory to God by our lives was shown by our Redeemer, Jesus of Nazareth, *the image of the unseen God, the first-born among many siblings.*[24] We are called among *the many siblings*, and leaving aside metaphors and comparisons, we now turn to him, who lived a life-arc as we live our life-arc: birth, maturation, mission, death. His human experience was, as is ours, a sharing in God's light and life on the earth. He did it, to our amazement, flawlessly and entirely, even faced with the worst of human travails and agonies.

We are told that *God decided beforehand who were those destined to be molded in the pattern [image] of His Son.*[25] So we find ourselves required to know about him. We must look to His experiences, to His sayings and actions, and even to His thoughts and yearnings and purposes. Reverently but boldly, we are to consider His perspectives, perceptions, desires, and much else, because we are *destined to be molded in His pattern*, and to accept this freely and intelligently.

Consideration:
The Word Became Flesh and Dwelt among Us

The People to whom Jesus came believed that God had created the world in seven days. We have no reason to think that they thought much about it; that was a philosophical question, and philosophy remained a pastime for the privileged. Further, Jesus' people thought that God had created the world as he wanted it to be, and they firmly believed *that whatever God does endures forever; nothing can be added to it, nor anything taken from it; God has done this, so that all should stand in awe before him.*[26]

As for belief about creation, Jesus left Revelation where he found it. If Jesus of Nazareth knew differently, it was because he was given knowledge not given to other humans—supernatural in the theological sense.[27] Surely Jesus experienced knowing things others did not know. His companions marveled at His knowledge, which they thought far beyond the norm. They could not distinguish—as we cannot know—what was astute assessment from what was supernaturally inspired.

Who could decide, for instance, whether it was revealed to Jesus that Nathaniel sat under a fig tree or whether he knew by some astute estimate of sense evidence? It doesn't much matter because we can't imitate or imagine how crystalline His human consciousness was—pure, without sinful prejudice or constraint. We are wiser pondering what he felt, valued, desired, and especially to watch what he enacted.

What Jesus of Nazareth enacted consistently was His purpose to convey God's loving and merciful presence to the People. His heart was eager to show them how to trust the Father absolutely. He will show that magnanimously at the end of His life. But all His life long, he had tried to bring them to feel how God's love is as great and as urgent as the rain and the sunlight.

⟳✺⟲

To go back to the beginning. A thousand years before Jesus—about three thousand years ago to us—the People of God had learned that God—their God—had created everything *in the beginning*. They believed that it had come to be *by the word of the Lord*; just by His *word his works are made*.[28] When the twelve tribes were still active, well before Jesus, the People saw that Word as a sort of emanation from God, standing somehow between God and creation. As the centuries passed, the People came to feel that the Word was somehow personal. In the Book of Wisdom, the Word speaks: *Before the mountains had been shaped, before the hills, I was brought forth*.[29] This was written in Greek in Jewish Alexandria during the Lady Mary's grandmother's time. By this time, the People believed that *When [God] established the heavens, I was there*—and Wisdom was somehow personal—a Person. The mature Jesus knew that he was, himself, at that beginning.

In what our tradition calls *the fullness of time*, God revealed what cannot otherwise be known to all who believe in him. We can hear this revelation about *the beginning* because he has given us the virtue, the power, and authority to declare as our own thinking and belief, from our own hearts, what His apostle John wrote:

> *In the beginning was the Word, and the Word was with God, and the Word was God. He was in the beginning with God.*
>
> *All things came into being through him, and without him not one thing came into being.*
>
> *The Word became flesh, he lived among us, and we saw his glory, the glory that he has from the Father as only Son of the Father, full of grace and truth.*

The Spirit of Life formed the humanity of Jesus of Nazareth. That same Spirit forms each human life today, just the way the sun would fill any mirror that had been aimed at it back then and does the same today. St. Paul told the Romans when some who had known Jesus were still alive: that *God had decided beforehand who were the ones destined to be molded to the pattern of his Son.*[30]

Here is what we hold: We are as we are because Jesus is as he is. Or to think historically: we are as we are because he was as he was—Jesus of Nazareth.

This is how Christ is our foundation. God is our "sun." As he was, so we are in God's image, the way the sun's image is in a mirror aimed at it. Not the whole sun, of course, but what of it the mirror can hold. So with us. To begin with, God *exists*—and so do we, in our limits. God exists as three distinct Persons—and so are all of us distinct from one another as persons. And as God is intelligent, free, creative, always relating—so are we: limited, but *in his image.*

More than that: Revelation also declares that we are created in God's *likeness.* How any of us could be *like* God seems impossible to imagine. It would be, except that Revelation also tells us that Jesus of Nazareth is *the visible image of the invisible God.* We are *created to His pattern,* and we can choose to take Him as our model who is both human and divine.

Now we know the response to the challenge that *anyone who claims to abide in Him ought to live as He lived.*[31] We learn how he lived, as the earliest disciples did, by considering the human experience of the Redeemer. His friends made this possible for us by writing down memories and stories, sayings and miracles—the things Jesus said and did.

So we come to obey the Lord: *Learn of me, for I am meek and humble,* He said.[32] And *I am the way, the truth, and the life.*[33] Really, we are doing no more than obeying Him when we consider the human experience of the Redeemer.

For Consideration

- The Son loved human creatures so much that He wanted to come live as we do.
- What do I appreciate about the theory of evolution in the light of revelation?

2

To Err Is Human
Luke 2

Context and Condition

Jesus lived in a definite place and time. Scholars have learned a lot about it. That place and time—that "context"—is the first thing to note when we think about His human experience.

Begin with Nazareth in Galilee, where he grew up. We have discovered that it was a small town of some 150 people. In Jesus' life, Galilee included a mountainous stretch in the north where the Jordan emptied into the lake. His parents lived further south, in *a country of hills and valleys watered by the rains of heaven.*[34] The people were deeply religious who devoutly believed of their land that *the eyes of Yahweh your God are always on it . . . from the beginning of the year to its end.* Nazareth itself was surrounded by hillside vineyards and had an irrigation system for the grain fields.

This made Galilee inviting, and invaders came. Over the centuries, it had been conquered in turns by the Assyrians, Babylonians, and Greeks. Thus Jesus was born into a mixed population, some still serving their own gods. The Romans had come in Joseph's grandparents' time, and when Joseph took Mary into his home, Galilee was governed by a Roman-appointed king, Herod Antipas. He was the tyrant who would murder John the Baptist and bolster Pilate's judgment on Jesus.

In Nazareth, Joseph and Mary lived in a population that was conservative in belief and practice. Joseph was respected as *an upright man*, and he and Mary lived faithfully what they understood of the mandates in Deuteronomy and Leviticus. We have every reason to think that they kept the holiness code and said the prayers. They dutifully taught Jesus proper behaviors according to the Law's command, *talking about them when you are at home and when you are away.*[35] *Teach them to your children, talking about them when you are at home and when you are away, when you lie down and when you rise.*

And they watched Jesus develop a notable interest in the Torah—the written and oral teachings—and a great reverence toward the Temple.[36] Joseph took the boy Jesus to synagogue on Sabbath to hear passages from the Torah—the Pentateuch, the prophets, and other books of the Bible—declaimed and interpreted. Jesus could cite a good deal of the writings. Later, he will say that people's readiness for the end time will be no more than *it was in the days of Noah* and *similarly, in the days of Lot.*[37] And he could say *you have heard it said* about a lot of things in the Pentateuch.[38]

Joseph brought the family to Jerusalem regularly. Every year, in the middle of the first month, he and Mary would take Jesus up to Jerusalem for the Feast of Passover. They would spend two nights on the road and walk as much as twenty miles a day. Winter rains were ending, and the moon was waxing to its full. As the pilgrimage group walked along, Mary and Joseph explained to Jesus that the People were celebrating the memory of God's saving them from slavery in Egypt, where they were kept safe by sprinkling the blood of a lamb on the doorposts of their homes.[39]

The year Jesus reached His majority, beginning His thirteenth year, the family was required to take him to the Temple in Jerusalem. All these years, Joseph had been responsible for his son's actions; now Jesus is responsible for himself. He is thought of as a man.

This is a good place to begin considering the human experience of the Redeemer. He is now able to sign contracts, and he can marry. He must make some real changes in His perspective on things, the way he perceives and values them. What he does now is likely to define His life's purpose and course.

Consideration: How Jesus Remains in the Temple

Their neighbors remembered that *when he was twelve years old, the family went up for the feast as usual.*[40] They were required to go this year because the boy has reached His majority. He knew that he was now responsible for His own ritual purity. So, on the way, he would not do what boys do, push away a dead lamb or pick up a dead bird. If he touched a corpse now, he would be ritually impure and responsible to bathe, after sundown but before joining the prayer at supper.

He knew these things, naturally, because Mary and Joseph talked about them. He knew them because men regularly gathered in groups—as they will around Jesus later in His life—to share memory of passages of the Torah and to discuss and debate whether we live after death and who is responsible for the children whose parents just died. Jesus carried all this in mind and heart to Jerusalem in this historic year in His life.

Jesus faced a choice all of us must face. He had one purpose in life: to love and serve the one God. As he grew and matured, he saw more than one way to do this. He felt cultural pressures, of course, like the expectation that a man should marry. It was not the only way. His cousin John was taking another.

John had *never drunk wine or strong drink* and has lived in God's Spirit from boyhood.[41] Now he was living like an ancient prophet in the desert. Jesus was thinking seriously about His cousin's way, as His later long stretch of days of fasting and prayer in the desert suggest. But Jesus was deeply attracted by and attached to the revealed word of God. He had heard a lot of it in synagogue. For five centuries, the text of the Pentateuch had been fixed. Now, in the minds of the strict, it was so holy that it should not even be translated from the Hebrew, though the language had faded among the ordinary people the way Latin has faded away among Catholics in our own time. But Jesus had heard teachers recite long passages of it, and he had a keen memory.

This Word of God was Israel's most holy treasure. And it was preserved best in the Temple, which, in Jesus' mind, was *my father's house*—the place where God would dwell in the kingdom. He decided to become a disciple of the teachers in Jerusalem. Through this relationship, he would have become a different man from the one he did become. But the Spirit prevented it.

The feast over, His parents set off for home with their friends. *They assumed he was somewhere in the party.*[42] Mary knew he could now join the men; Joseph knew that he might stay for a while with His younger friends near their mothers. In the evening, *they went to look for him among their relations and acquaintances.* They didn't find him. Parents will know what terror gripped their hearts that night and as they walked the next day's long walk back *to Jerusalem to search for him.*

After another miserable night, on the third morning, they went to the Temple. They found him sitting among the teachers, listening to them, and asking them questions.

Jesus valued the Word as an inexhaustible treasure. He seems to have absorbed everything he heard about God's Word. At twelve, he was a prodigy—*all those who heard him were astounded at His understanding and His answers.* And he asked them questions that stunned them. Jesus was not playing trivial pursuit. For he was listening to Revelation to find His self.

We often think that we have to invent ourselves. But the truth is different. Our true self is our appreciative memory of our past in our context as it has brought us to be in the present and as we look to our future. Jesus was listening to the People's history to find His place in it—the place that the Father had been preparing for him among the People.

That's what he was doing when His parents came into the Court of the Gentiles and were overwhelmed seeing him there. His mother blurted *out why had He done this. Look how worried your father and I have been, looking for you.* He replied, *Why were you looking for me? Did you not know that I must be in my Father's house?* But *they did not understand what he meant.*

We cannot reasonably believe that he had never talked with Joseph about doing this. That negligence would have been sinfully irresponsible. Plainly, the conversation was not understood on both sides in the same sense. Is this a familiar occurrence in a family? Doesn't it sometimes happen that we think we understand one another—until we do something that makes it clear that we did *not* understand one another? So *they did not understand what He meant,* and he stayed and they had to hurry, searching frantically.

None of the three sinned: not Jesus, not Mary, and not Joseph. All three suffered, and the boy had a harsh experience of doing what he thought right, failing, and hurting His parents. That weighed heavily on him on the long walk back to Nazareth.

But God the Father took this misadventure, painful as it was for all three, and made a grace of it, as His friends will come to understand: *For the high priest we have is not incapable of feeling our weaknesses with us, but has been put to the test in exactly the same way as ourselves, apart from sin.*[43]

Even being pained and tested by a serious mistake.

For Consideration

- What was it like for the boy Jesus when it hit him that he had caused His parents real suffering?
- What does it matter to me that Jesus of Nazareth—and His parents—made mistakes?

3

The People of God in Jesus' Day
Matthew 3

Context and Condition

As Jesus grew up in "Galilee of the Gentiles," he surely would have heard gentile boys name other gods. But he was taught that there is one God who is God of all the other gods. With a devout mother and an upright father, he readily made His own a faith in the one true God.

Every one of us who grew up in a Christian family did that. Surrounded by faith, we might not have been much tempted, but we still had to develop our own faith. Jesus surely did. We are explicitly told that he grew not only in *age*, but also in the *grace* and the *wisdom* revealed to His People.[44] As Karl Rahner insisted, we can "speak without any embarrassment of a spiritual, indeed religious, development of Jesus."[45]

As Jesus matured and heard more and more about how God had dealt with His People, he learned that gentiles seemed to decide which gods to call on. But His People had not chosen their God. Their God had chosen them to be *my treasured possession out of all the peoples*.[46] Even with gentiles living among them, the People kept themselves apart: *I have separated you from the other peoples to be mine.*[47]

Hundreds of years before anyone was writing things down, they had known the Ten Commandments and many other laws. They had known that sacrificing their infants was a pagan *abomination*. They had known prostitution and adultery were not human foibles but grave affronts to the Holy God. They knew not to cheat or lie or to swear falsely, *swearing falsely by my name, profaning the name of your God. I am the Lord.*[48]

Jesus grew up aware that the whole People were holy. For God had instructed Moses: *Speak to the whole congregation of the people of Israel and say to them: You shall be holy, for I the Lord your God am holy.*[49] The whole People are holy, destined to live according to the Law. For several centuries, the *statutes and ordinances* had been handed down parent to child, scribe to synagogue: No images of the one God. Honor parents and the elderly. Leave some part of the harvest for the needy, the poor, and the refugee.

This was the oral tradition that Jesus lived with. The Pharisees tried to live it meticulously. The Sadducees looked down on it, trusting the written tradition alone. Jesus, himself, heard the voice of the Father: *You shall keep all my statutes and all my ordinances, and observe them: I am the Lord.*[50] He learned, though, that human willfulness gets into *statutes and ordinances*, causing divisions to begin. This was the source of the fierce arguments and conflicts that Jesus ran into as he came into public life.[51]

In His maturity, Jesus was among those whose *delight is in the law of the Lord, and on his law they meditate day and night.*[52] He had thought and prayed into the heart of the Law. And as he grew older, he became more aware of how badly things were going. Orphans and widows were not always cared for. The poor suffered without relief. Many slaves lived hopeless among them. They had heard no prophet since Zechariah and Malachi, more than four hundred years ago.

Priests and religious leaders argued and left things—the land and the People—unsettled. Some of the People right around Galilee were calling on other gods for rain and a good harvest.

Yet the Spirit kept in the People's memory the declaration of the last prophet in Israel, Malachi: *Behold, I will send you Elijah the prophet, before the coming of the great and terrible day of the Eternal.*[53]

Then John the Baptist came off the desert, baptizing. And Jesus will later tell His disciples that His cousin John was the *Elijah who is to come*—the one promised by the prophet Malachi.[54] Perhaps already convinced of that, he went to find His cousin at the Jordan.

Consideration: The Redeemer Baptized among Sinners

How beautiful on the mountains are the feet of the messenger announcing peace, of the messenger of good news . . . who proclaims salvation and says to Zion, "Your God is King."[55]

Isaiah prophesied this of the Messiah, the One to come. Unhappily, many of the sinful listeners were not much interested in the message of the One to come. So His cousin John was busy fulminating judgment on the careless. Did the People not repent of their sins, he roared, *even now the axe is being laid at the root of the trees.*[56]

Jesus knew that this fierce judgment echoed around Galilee. Plenty of gentiles with their temples were tempting the People to do business with them. Jesus may not have known the names of the conquerors of "Galilee of the Gentiles," but he knew that Babylonians and Assyrians, Greeks and Romans had brought their gods onto the fertile land and were testing the People's trust in the one true God. He would see pagan practices—gestures and amulets and mutterings—all around him.

And Jesus knew the People's desolation, that they felt far from God, all together unholy and unclean. It is a human experience we know well now, when our nation is full of angry divisions.

Consecrated rituals of cleanness were widespread, ritual bathing important among them. "Baptizing" helped those who felt less unworthy to belong among the Chosen, close to the all-holy God. There were "mikvahot"—baths for cleansing—dug into the earth under homes all over the Holy Land. Their still water for cleansing guilt and shame was always ready. But *living water* was most effective: the lake or the river Jordan.

It was at the Jordan that John had come, *in the desert preaching a baptism of repentance for the forgiveness of sins.*[57] His cousin Jesus had been with him in the desert, where he had grown convinced through prayer and fasting and severe temptations that he was not to be a prophet like John. What he knew about himself when he came to the Jordan was that he was to be a teacher, *to announce peace and declare salvation.* And he came to the Jordan already aware of having power beyond ordinary over things and spirits, powers that were not magic but throbbed in His faith and trust in Israel's God.

Woven tightly into His matured human character was His love for the all-powerful God as *Father.* Jesus knew God not as an awesome absence, but as *Father.* He prayed out loud many times, *Father, I thank you.* His work here was to help the People know that God, *the Father*, has reconciled himself to His children.

John had come to appreciate His cousin's destiny. While John has been sent to demand repentance, Jesus is sent to bring healing and forgiveness. He comes bringing reconciliation; he *is* reconciliation. And now he is standing at the shore, among the sinners? So as Jesus takes His turn to step into the water to be immersed and purified, the astonished John blurts out: *"I baptize YOU?"*

We might wonder what Jesus meant by standing among the sinful at the Jordan. He was always clear that he did what the Father wanted. How could he know what guilt and uncleanness do to the human spirit?

Well, he wanted to know. He already felt empathy for the guilty and shamed. When still a boy, he had perceived that other children felt guilt and chose guile, which he did not feel or choose. But loving them, he empathized with them. He *gets* their sin and guilt; he *knows* their regret and remorse. This matured into His compassion for people who abused themselves and one another—and for religious leaders who were confounded by the Law. He was still learning all of this when He stood at the Jordan.

He plainly yearned for closeness. He chose to be near the real people to whom he had been sent. He did not want to seem to witness to people in general. He wanted to know how to hold in His heart the ones he talked to. So he decided he would go and be among the sinners. *Then Jesus came from Galilee to John at the Jordan to be baptized by him.*[58]

John stopped him and did not want to go through what seemed to him an empty ritual. *"I need to be baptized by you, and yet you are coming to me?"* But Jesus felt that being baptized as a sinner would *fulfill all righteousness.* He had set himself to honor the covenant and keep the holy Law, down to the smallest detail. And the real Law calls first for love of God and then, with that same love, love of neighbor. So John immersed him in the living waters.

When he stood there drenched, he saw *the heavens open* and *the Spirit of God descending like a dove coming upon him.* Then everyone heard a voice: *"This is my beloved Son, with whom I am well pleased."*[59]

Jesus resonates with that voice. He has chosen to stand with fornicators and thieves, and now he knows that the Father approves of His choice. He feels deeply consoled and confirmed in His epochal decision about His purpose: *I have come not to judge the world but to save the world.*[60] He begins His work by showing us where it must start.

Now he has experienced something very ordinary in the world He has come to save. Standing with any group of people is standing with sinners. He has come simply as one of us—all of whom know ourselves sinners.

The consequence is clear. We don't go to our own Jordan to find out that we are sinners. We know that our life in this kingdom of earth is interwoven with sin, warp and woof. When we go to our Jordan, we might find standing in front of us is the One who need not be here but is.

If we are humble, we will feel as surprised as was His cousin John.

For Consideration

- I ponder what was in Jesus' mind and heart as He waited in line to be baptized.
- If I were in line to be baptized at the Jordan behind Jesus, which of my sins would urgently need cleansing?

4

How It Was as He Began His Work
Matthew 4

Context and Condition

Jesus of Nazareth understood himself well after three decades of *growing in wisdom, age, and grace*. We cannot know His divine mind, but we do know that he had great human gifts and that he learned through "education, experience, relationships with other men . . . by his human reflection about the world, men, and God."[61] Just like us.

As Jesus moved into public life, he knew through years of reflection and prayer that he was to have a special place in the history of the People and that he was living in that place. He also felt that God's Spirit gave him the authority to speak His own mind and heart about the things of God, to interpret the true practice of the Law, and to reveal its deepest meaning.

The mature disciple grasps that we show ourselves most completely in our doings. When we humans act, we *enact* what is in our minds and hearts—this is what Jesus meant by the *tree bearing its fruit*.[62] So we really begin to know the human experience of Jesus of Nazareth when he begins His work. And His *good tree bears good fruit*.

We should note that we can imagine His human experience because each of us has *grown in wisdom, age, and grace* as he did. The Son of God embraced the slow process of coming-to-be a mature adult, the process we all go through. He was an infant and grew aware that there were others who were not himself. A boy, a youth, a young man, he grew into language and thought and learned to reflect on His experiences. We know only a few of His experiences from His early years. We know a good deal about him as a mature man.

We might face a lurking issue. As human as Jesus' *growing* was, and as like ours as it was, we might still hesitate to ask about the Redeemer's intimate thoughts and feelings. He is the Son of God, after all, and somehow it seems irreverent to probe. However completely he was human, he was also as completely divine. So we have reason to be respectful and modest even as we believe that we are as we are because Jesus was as he was.

Clearly, the "imitation of Christ" calls on us to know him more clearly and love him more dearly. And it will help to consider that this imitation raises to the order of grace what is a basic human process. We are so created that we learn to be ourselves by imitating others.

We imitate their words and learn language. Along with those words and the whole language, we also learn to imitate feelings and gestures, and even the desires they express. We naturally learn to be like others and on the way, we also find how we will differ. At the completion of this process, we learn that we are unique and unrepeatable—yet, in many ways, *like* many others.

The "imitation of Christ," however, comes not from our human nature but from our nature's Creator. God has revealed to us that we are made in His image and likeness. And God has shown us His "likeness" in the *visible image of the invisible God*, Jesus of Nazareth.[63] We will imitate him only by hearing and considering how he enacted all His own gifts as the Spirit moved him.

As though to quell all our doubts, Jesus insisted: *Learn of Me, because I am meek and humble of heart.*[64] And he told us, *I am the way, the truth, and the life.*[65] He spoke from His heart when He told His three closest friends, stunned while watching Him transfigured: *Do not be afraid.*[66]

So we really come to know Jesus as he does *the works that the Father sent me to do.*[67] As he does them, he tells the crowds how he sees things, His perspective on them. He says what he sees, how he perceives the human world around him. He shows to His friends what he values and what he wants.

Thank God that we have a good record of a good bit of that. So we begin again our own work: to know him more clearly, love him more dearly, and follow him more nearly, as long as we live, day by day.

Consideration: Jesus' Experiences as He Begins His Work

Jesus came to the People with *Good News*—but it was not quite the news many of them were waiting for. He felt the need for caution, having grown up hearing talk about a great savior—a king like David or a great prophet like Moses. He knew that this dream endured among the People in Galilee.

He would find that it endured in Judea to the south, too. Even at the end, after all His cautions, a crowd in Jerusalem will shout at their Savior riding on a donkey: *Blessed is the kingdom of our father David that is coming! Hosanna in the highest!*[68] They are still waiting for the great king.

He also knew that in Galilee, "Zealots" contended that the kingdom coming meant that the People would take up arms and drive out the Romans. They trusted God who *rescued us from our foes.*[69] Jesus knew some Zealots well; he would include one in His Twelve.

Facing the kind of charged atmosphere that we are familiar with, Jesus works to understand how His supernatural powers mesh with the People's need to freely accept Good News. He had to ponder what John's prophecy meant that *He will baptize you with the Holy Spirit and fire.*[70]

He surely had powers. Jesus appreciated them as confirmation of His authority to proclaim the Good News and forgive sins. He would tell some who would not believe His word to *believe the works that I do.*[71] He could use them to win a great political following or to make himself famous and powerful. The thought may seem absurd now, but he had to discern how and when to use these powers.

He would later humbly tell some of His disciples how he made sure that he would be both generous and selfless. Led *by the Spirit*, he went into the desert and *fasted for forty days and forty nights.*[72] During that time, he was *tempted by the devil* about using these powers. It seems hard to believe that our Holy Redeemer could have been tempted. But he was.

Jesus had felt that he was not to use these powers for His own benefit. But by now *he was famished* and so *the tempter came to Him.* You're famished. These rocks look like loaves. Why not? You have this power. And you're famished. Who will notice? Why not?

But Jesus appreciated bread most deeply as a gift from God, and bread for him was *every word that comes from the mouth of God.*

The tempter kept at it—as the tempter always does. So, you are going to bear the whole burden of leading this People, lifelong, unfailingly. You are sure to take the place of the Temple. You can certainly trust yourself. Take whatever risks you face, *for it is written, "He will command his angels concerning you,"* so jump off the Temple and be safe.

But Jesus had grown in wisdom and grace and knew very well that to trust himself instead of God was to *put the Lord our God to the test*— a fool's mistake that he will not make. He trusts the Father, especially now, when he feels most empty and weak. So he waits.

He trusts the Father by accepting the prophecies that he is to be a suffering king, meek and humble, unlike any king before him. The tempter thinks that being meek and humble is a weakness. Here's a place where he can get at Jesus. So *the devil took him to a very high mountain and showed him all the kingdoms of the world and their splendor; and he said to him, All these I will give you, if you will fall down and worship me.*

Jesus' choice is steady: His faith is in the one true God, *maker of heaven and earth.* He will bow down to no creature, not even for the whole world. *Jesus said to him, Away with you, Satan! for it is written, Worship the Lord your God, and serve only him.* He has made His choice and is faithful.

With that, Jesus left the desert and *suddenly angels came and waited on him* and He ate and drank the People's gifts from the Father.[73]

When Jesus reached the area at the Jordan where John had been baptizing, He *heard that John had been arrested, and he withdrew to Galilee.* He first went home to Nazareth. He had been gone for some months and returned so gaunt from dry days in the desert that some people hardly recognized *Joseph's son.* He stayed for some days and *went to the synagogue on the sabbath day, as was his custom.*[74] He was invited to read and found the prophecy of Isaiah about His own coming. Then he said, *Today this scripture has been fulfilled in your hearing.*[75] But it did not go well with the people of this small town He had thought to begin His ministry at home. Now he humbly left where he was no longer wanted. Now the *Son of Man has nowhere to lay his head.*[76]

Instead, he *made his home in Capernaum by the lake,* where trade flourished along the *Via Maris,* the main road to the sea. Perhaps a more sophisticated urban populace would be more open to the wonderful changes he was urging. Later, disciples would see the move as the fulfillment of a prophecy: *Land of Zebulun, land of Naphtali, on the road by the sea, across the Jordan, Galilee of the Gentiles—the people who sat in darkness have seen a great light.*[77] But that's not how it started.

There in Capernaum's synagogue, Jesus really begins the work the Father has given him: proclaiming *Repent, for the kingdom of heaven has come near.* Very near, His disciples later realized. For in Jesus, God in Person, is establishing the kingdom in quiet power, directly, meekly, and irresistibly.

In the desert, he had definitively accepted that it was not given him to establish the kingdom in any of the ways that His contemporaries imagined. Instead, he begins to imagine himself a farmer sowing seed. He sprinkles and waits. He works for God's kingdom the way a woman works bread with yeast: fold it in, fold it in, and wait.[78] He has learned to value His work as a beginning—like a little mustard seed—a farmer plants it; it grows.[79] The kingdom will certainly grow; but He knows that it will grow like wheat in a field in which an enemy has sown weeds.[80]

While His heart is set on beginning the kingdom, Jesus begins looking for the ones whom the Father has given him to continue His work.

For Consideration

- What does His *meek and humble heart* tell about how Jesus appreciated His human experience?
- Jesus considered His place in the history of the People and the kingdom. What do I consider mine?

5

Jesus, and Some Pharisees, under a Hole in the Roof
Luke 5, Mark 2

Context and Condition

The Pharisees were men who lived an upright, Law-abiding life. A party of laymen and scribes, they were all over Galilee and Judea and in the Diaspora, too. There were other groups—Sadducees were a priestly party concentrated in Jerusalem, and some Zealots had withdrawn into desert enclaves—but the Pharisees were commonly the religious leaders of their places.

They were imbued with feelings of specialness and felt the great dignity of having been chosen as His own by the one true God. They felt that the People must live "clean" and "pure" and expect to please God, as *day after day they seek me and delight to know my ways.*[81] They followed—many of them scrupulously—the special ways that tradition had handed on to them: honoring the Sabbath, daily prayers, days of fasting, and washing constantly to be "clean." And in the end, they hoped for a resurrection in eternal life.

There were some about whom Isaiah had chided, *you serve your own interest on your fast-day*, oppress your workers, and *fast only to quarrel and to fight.*[82] The People had no hierarchy, but Pharisees had earned a certain position, which had led to privilege and wealth. We can expect that enough of them came to like privilege and wealth and became self-satisfied and vain. And plenty of the Pharisees performed their "uprightness" of almsgiving, prayer, and fasting publicly.

But they were a serious movement in Jesus' day. Perhaps in Joseph's great-grandfather's time, the Pharisees had begun earnestly teaching the People to worship God where they were and not wait until they could go to the Temple. They insisted that praying and studying the Law served God as much as bloody sacrifices did. And they promoted having synagogues in every town.

In general, Pharisees were set on the search for holiness, as was Jesus Himself. Jesus had surely known Pharisees as He grew into His maturity and made Capernaum His city. He began announcing in the synagogue His Good News that God reigns now, *already*, today. Religious leaders on all sides promptly heard about His message, and they promptly wondered about Him.

One obvious possibility was that God had raised up another prophet like John the Baptist, whom Herod had killed. Or one of the older prophets—maybe Elijah, whom the prophet Malachi had promised? Everyone was aware that, until John the Baptist, God had sent no prophet after the long-dead Malachi—and now John is silenced, beheaded by Herod. The most devout, especially, were keen to know about this Galilean.

Jesus, in His turn, is keen to have the opinion leaders hear Him and believe His message. They are key to the People's beliefs, and He respects their leadership and position. He discerned early in His ministry how rigidity in practices can hide something else: the need for recognizing sin and repenting. He knows hypocrisy.

He will show that He has no desire to get into the debating that they love. He wants to honor these men. And He earnestly hopes that each of them might *decide for themselves what is right*, and experience the Law in freedom, changing their perspectives and perceptions, what they really value and desire.[83]

Jesus hopes that they, along with everyone else, will experience the Way in freedom.

Consideration: Jesus Instructs Some Pharisees

Jesus has returned from one of the many trips He will make around the towns and villages of Galilee. He is at home in Capernaum, preaching to a mixed crowd, because people had come *from every village of Galilee and Judea and from Jerusalem.*[84] Some Pharisees were in the crowded room because people were saying that Jesus' teaching was new, with authority behind it.[85]

The scribes wanted to hear what Jesus had to say about the Law. He had made His belief clear: *anyone whose uprightness does not surpass that of the scribes and Pharisees will never get into the kingdom of heaven.*[86] Well, if uprightness is not keeping the Law, what is it? What is this *Repent* and *Good News*—and what does it have to do with healing people and driving out demons?

Jesus honored holiness, but He believed with the People that everyone was born guilty, *a sinner when my mother conceived me.*[87] But He judged that the scribes put too much emphasis on guilt for breaking the Law. By Jesus' day, scribes and teachers of the Law argued endlessly about which was the greatest among the commandments—and they had counted four hundred.

Jesus saw that they had eroded their understanding of sin. They made it a physical matter between each one and the all-just God. They were ignoring what the Father demanded of us in our relationships with those nearest us and even with the stranger. They leaned toward fear and away from love.

Jesus has chosen not to live in that mindset. He has come to help the People see that sin is not an external matter like dirt on the hands;

sin is evil in the heart out of which bad acts come. And sin is not only between each one and God. Sin is *among* us, in any action not rooted in love in our hearts. For the Father is offended when any of us is unloving—or unjust or hateful or negligent—to even the littlest among us. These are the wrongs we must repent of.

Jesus loved the Law and never intended to deny any of the prophets. But He saw that vanity and pride, riches and power, had cemented over the deeper meaning of the prophets' words. His Good News demanded careful attention because, as good as it is for us, it does not begin with us. It begins with the Father.

God the Father has reconciled Himself to humankind's sinfulness, as the Torah tells and prophets have insisted on. Jesus has come because the Father wants the People to know that they are forgiven when they turn to Him, always. *As a mother comforts her child, so I shall comfort you.*[88]

This Good News challenged many of the People's cherished beliefs and practices. Jesus knew that it was a lot to teach. We can be tempted to believe that faith in Christ is simple. But the mature know that faith demands constant reflection and conversion of heart.

When Jesus came back to Capernaum this time, and the scribes and Pharisees gathered to listen to Him, He was given an excellent occasion to invite conversion of heart. This is what happened.

In the crowded room in Peter's house, many were gathered together, *so that there was no longer room for them, not even about the door.*[89] A commotion broke out at the door, but Jesus kept teaching. The commotion, it turned out, involved a paralytic carried by four friends, who had not come just to listen to Jesus.

They had heard not only of His teaching but also of His works of healing. Four of them were big enough and had strong enough convictions of mind and heart—that they had come to bring their afflicted friend to where Jesus was teaching. There, they showed how strong their conviction was that Jesus will heal their friend. Everything points to confidence and trust—the paralytic's willingness to be hauled off, the four's determination to get him to Jesus, strong enough to make them do something a little mad.

They removed the roof above Jesus' head. And when they had made a big enough opening, they let down the pallet on which the paralytic lay. Jesus sees this bag coming down before Him and sees that it's a body. But what He notices is their faith, the faith of all five of them. And He has no trouble discerning what they want. They are asking for it in an undeniable way.

So, He decides and says to the paralytic, "*My son, your sins are forgiven.*" The effects are immediate. The paralytic feels motion in his body. The scribes and Pharisees are stunned: Who can forgive sins but God alone? They say nothing, but Jesus is keenly sensitive. He could see the strong reaction to this *your sins are forgiven*. Some of His followers would later remember that He had perceived them having "wicked" thoughts—sitting there, questioning in their hearts, *Why does this fellow speak in this way? It is blasphemy!* Other followers remembered only that perceiving in His spirit that *they thus questioned within themselves*, Jesus could see that they were trapped in their own interpretations of The Law, some more rigidly than others.

Jesus gently asks them all to consider: *"Why do you have these thoughts in your hearts?"* He respected their knowledge of The Torah, where it is only God who forgives sin. But now the Father wants to share the divine forgiveness with His creatures. Jesus must help them grasp and accept that. Later on, Jesus will proclaim explicitly: *if you do not forgive others, neither will your Father forgive your trespasses.*[90] But for now, He must help these scribes and Pharisees open their minds and hearts to a profound change.

Only God can forgive sins? And who but God can heal a paralytic by command? Then Jesus makes His point by turning to the paralytic and saying quietly: *"I order you: get up, pick up your stretcher, and go off home."* And the man does it, right in front of them. Jesus hopes His *which is easier* will have opened minds and hearts—at least a little.

Now Jesus has done what only God can do. He knows that he has much more to teach His people. But for now, He waits to see who will believe in Him enough to carry on this work when He is gone.

For Consideration

- What was in Jesus' mind and heart as he said, *I order you: pick up your stretcher and go home?*
- Ponder whether God does great works today that encourage us to turn to him.

PART TWO

MOVING STRONG IN PROCLAIMING THE GOOD NEWS

6

The Human Character
of the Redeemer
John 2

Context and Condition

Human character is the habitual set of attitudes and actions that we present to our lifeworld. The habits are not merely external but express the strengths and weaknesses, the virtues and flaws that make us who we are.

Jesus had a human character. One of the scribes described it for Him: *"Teacher, we know that you are sincere, and teach the way of God in accordance with truth, and show deference to no one; for you do not regard people with partiality."*[91] So "we know"—that is, everyone can see this—that Jesus was sincere, truthful, self-assured, and took each person as that person was. That was His character; He was known this way.

Jesus freely developed His human character; it was part of His *coming from the Father*, His *humbling Himself*. It began taking shape as the Lady Mary taught Him words and how to pray with them. She and Joseph explained to Him various human behaviors, such as a child is likely to ask about. And Joseph modeled upright manhood for Jesus to imitate, so He could grow into *the carpenter's son*—whose character everyone recognized. Or thought they did.

In a way, we can understand that Jesus had to develop a human character. For before He could authentically instruct others, Jesus had to experience *discerning for Himself what was right, acceptable, and perfect.*[92] He had to *make his own tree good* so as to produce the good fruit of many virtues.

As we consider His human experience, we will note many of His virtues, as the scribe did so casually. But He lived some less-often named virtues that are worth noting here:

- *Uprightness* is a virtue we do not much attend to now. In Jesus' day, the upright followed the Law faithfully, feeling their place in the history of God's People. Jesus loved the Law, and His character showed what the fulfilled Law looked like. For instance, He knew that *Sabbath was made for man*, not vice versa, so when he healed on the Sabbath, He was showing how to obey the heart of the Law.

- *Meekness* is strength refrained, power kept close. Jesus showed this when He was rejected in Nazareth and when He left the fearful Gadarenes. The Lord named *meekness* as a leading virtue in His own character: *learn of me because I am meek and humble.*

- *Generosity* characterizes the person who gives openhandedly to others—food or other material things where these are appropriate; or learning, ideas, and convictions; or care, affection, loyalty, and love—and who feels well rewarded simply in giving. Think of the multiplication of bread. And note that Jesus did not heal crowds or groups. He healed *individuals*—anyone who asked.

- *Docility* in a child is openness to being taught and shaped. Mature adults are docile when we can read a situation well, are ready to learn from events, and respond intelligently to reality. Jesus showed this at Cana, as we will see.

It happened this way. Jesus has just begun gathering disciples, and they are getting to know one another. They go with the Lady Mary to a wedding feast in the village of Cana, a few hours' walk north from Nazareth. Sometime before the day of the feast, the groom had gone to the bride's father and given him a wedding gift, which confirmed the betrothal. This was the first step in a marriage.

The second step comes on the day of this feast. The bride's family—marriages were arranged by families, not by the couple—has dressed her carefully and leads her to her new home. The groom now receives his bride and then invites everyone to a feast. It will last some days, during which Jesus will reveal something significant about His human character.

Consideration: How Jesus Discerns a Second Time at Cana

By the time of the wedding in Cana, Jesus may not yet have taught in the synagogue in Nazareth, or He may already have exhorted Capernaum to *repent and believe Good News*. We know that when He goes to Cana with His mother and some new disciples, He has not yet made sure His disciples understand the significance of His powers over nature and the spirits. The remark He will make to His mother suggests that He has not yet performed works of power.

At Cana, the party is fine—until the wine begins to run out. Running out of wine at a wedding feast would be an embarrassment in any culture. In Jesus' culture, the bridegroom and his family will be painfully shamed and for the rest of their lives will be known as the couple who ran out of wine at their wedding.

The Lady Mary senses what the waiters are noting, and she is keenly aware of everything this means. So, *the mother of Jesus said to him, They have no wine*. A sensitive man, Jesus promptly feels all of what His mother is alluding to. But quietly self-aware, He says to her, *My dear lady, what do you want of me? My hour has not yet come*.[93]

As far as anyone who told this story remembered, Jesus' mother said nothing further. She knew that her son was docile; He had gone with her and His father from the Temple back to Nazareth. Once back there, He had continued living as a working man, at least for a time with His father Joseph, but in any case, for as long as the common understanding of *honor your parents* required. For Jesus was, like His father, *an upright man.*[94]

And He has grown into a docile adult, able to accept the realities in a situation for what they are and to deal with them creatively. Here are these spouses on a day as important to them as any other will ever be, about to be deeply shamed. Jesus feels the threat hanging over them on the most joyful day of their lives. Humbly refusing to feel put-upon, He discerns that it is time to let circumstance matter. He lets the needs of the people shape His desiring. He is learning that what the Father wants Him to do will often enough come to Him as others' needs and desires.

He had discerned before Cana that *his hour had not yet come*, which was quite a consequential decision. His disciples were not ready. Now He chooses not to cling to His discernment. He lets go of a prior discernment—an act of the meekness that marks a strong character.

The Lady Mary sees that He will act so she says to the waiters, *"Do whatever he tells you."* Jesus has contemplated God's inexhaustible generosity in creation—the rain and the flowers, the splendid variety of peoples. Aware of His own splendor as a creature being made in the *image and likeness* of God, He decides what to do. *Fill the jars*, He tells them, *to the brim*. And then: *Now draw some out and take it to the steward.*[95]

Then He and His disciples watch a little drama, half comic and half hard to believe. The waiters draw some wine from the jars and bring it to the steward. He tastes it, and his surprise is tinted with anger. He then brings this new wine for the bridegroom to taste. He rather tartly points out that normal people serve the better wine as the feast begins, and *when everyone has drunk freely*, they then bring out the poorer stuff. *But you have kept the good wine until now.*

Decades later, some of His disciples will remember this as *the first of his signs.*[96] It showed that a power greater than any normal human power was at work. It was a clear sign: *six stone jars . . . each holding twenty or thirty gallons.* That's a lot of good wine.

The jars mean everything to the wedding party. They all will have *drunk freely* yet again, with plenty left over. This great plenty runs the risk of excess; people do not always know when to stop *drinking freely*. But Jesus runs this risk—just as the Creator runs it, over and over. Our Creator is unremittingly extravagant—a cosmos of billions of suns, without limit; and on this planet, immense flocks of birds, fields full of tiny flowers and heavy heads of barley and wheat. And of course, billions of beautiful people—and always sunlight falling on everyone.

Hence, the One who *came from the Father into the world* joyfully risked being generous.[97] Jesus of Nazareth experiences the Reign of God as generous, superabundant, a splendid plenty. For Him, the Reign is a great banquet. It's a big event unfolding in crowds; sometimes everyone invited to eat. *Go out into the roads and lanes, and compel people to come in, so that my house may be filled.*[98]

In the likeness of God, the Redeemer's character is marked by generosity. How many baskets left over? Seven? Twelve? He knows in His own heart the reward given to the generous: *give, and it will be given to you; good measure, pressed down, shaken together, running over, will be put into your lap.*[99]

At Cana in Galilee, the Father responds with magnanimity to the Son's generosity. For *his disciples believed in him;* they are given a depth of faith that Jesus has not thought they were ready for.[100] In His prudence, He has hardly expected something different, and His discernment has been clear: do not push them yet. But the Father always surprises. And we can rightly surmise that, to Jesus' delight, everyone is in a very good mood by the end of the feast.

For Consideration

- How did Jesus view this dilemma: the disciples are not ready, but the couple needs me now.
- I examine how generously I set aside my agenda to meet others' needs.

7

The Redeemer's Experience of God
Matthew 6

Context and Condition

Scholars study the human experience of Jesus objectively. They study life in the Holy Land during Jesus' lifetime: daily life, religious practice, marriage customs, farming, commerce, and a lot more. What they teach helps us place Jesus in His time, as one individual among many similar individuals.

When we pray, though, we turn to the Person, Jesus of Nazareth. We are not studying Him as a Galilean, a workman, one of the last prophets—those and other categories count individuals. We are asking to know and love a Person who may belong in all those categories but who is more than the sum of all of them. Furthermore, we believe that Jesus is both a human and divine Person—a thrilling, incomprehensible identity and mystery.

And when we prayerfully consider the human experience of the Redeemer, we are asking Him how he *was put to the test in exactly the same way as we ourselves, apart from sin.*[101] We are asking how He was "like us," and to do that, we have to bring our own experience to our prayer. We cannot avoid that, even when we think of Jesus' relationship with the Father.

We cannot ignore His intimate relationship with the Father. For every human being has as intimate a relationship with our Creator and Lord as we have with the earth's gravity. Unhappily, many of us give no more attention to God than we give to gravity. Jesus lived entirely attentive to the Father. As the biblical scholar Raymond Brown put it: "There is not a word in the gospels to indicate that at any state of his life Jesus was not aware of a unique relationship with God."[102]

His disciples could see His closeness to the Father in everything He did—all His enactments. Jesus said this clearly: *For the Father loves the Son, and shows him all that he himself is doing.*[103] What the Son was doing expressed His all-encompassing purpose in life: doing God's will.

But as we do, Jesus had to discern, day by day, and all day long. He could trust His impulses and desires because they were not skewed by sin; He had never violated His own conscience. Thus, He was free in desire and judgment, in emotion and thought. That is the freedom St. Paul says we are ourselves called to: *for freedom Christ has set us free.*[104] Reaching this state of freedom is what self-mastery is about, and what our struggles against passionate attachments are about.

Jesus discerned readily, but we mustn't think that His ready discernment made things easy. He will discern, for instance, that he must wait until Lazarus dies and then weep with His sisters. And His discernment is done in prayer.

This prayerfulness was one of Jesus' characteristics that His disciples remembered. They remembered Him praying often in public or off by Himself alone. His disciples remembered, for instance, that one time: *After he had dismissed the crowds, he went up into the hills by himself to pray.*[105] And one typical morning in Capernaum: a great while before day, he rose and went out to a lonely place, and there he prayed.[106] They also remembered that He sometimes prayed through the night: In these days he went out into the hills to pray; and all night he continued in prayer to God.[107]

Was He always in what St. Ignatius called consolation? Never tired? Down? We can't think that, for He shared two things about His own prayer when He remarked later to friends *that they ought to pray always and not lose heart.*[108] We can be confident that He *prayed always*, and that He knew what *losing heart* was like.

Jesus' prayer was His own, but prayer was entirely common among the People because God was close to them. Devout Jews prayed three times a day, not at fixed times as do the Muslims or as Catholics do with thrice-daily *Angelus*. Jesus shared prayer with His disciples. Prayer together was a regular feature of the life of Jesus' disciples from the beginning.[109] That's a beautiful habit we can well imitate.

They had all prayed with synagogue presidents, perhaps using one of the many formulaic prayers or psalms. And as we would expect, His disciples saw abuses. They had all witnessed *the hypocrites; for they love to stand and pray in the synagogues and at the street corners, that they may be seen by others.*[110] When His disciples asked what He thought about it, Jesus attended to their response. He began by saying that they do not need to *heap up empty phrases as the unbelievers do*, for the children of the Father know deep in their hearts that the *Father knows what you need before you ask him.*[111]

Then He taught them a prayer they could share together. But He went on to point to something He had been modeling for them, so that *as He has done, so we should also do*. He taught them about their private prayer.

Speaking from His own experience, Jesus said: *"But when you pray"*—this *you* is the singular, about each of His followers personally— *"you go into your room and shut the door and pray to your Father who is in secret; and your Father who sees in secret will reward you."*[112]

That's what we're doing now. And we like to end our times of prayer with the words the Lord Jesus taught them, enumerating for them the few things that He considered adequate to a person's daily prayer.

Consideration: How the Lord Prays to the Father

"Through his very bodily condition he sums up in himself the elements of the material world. Through him they are thus brought to their highest perfection and can raise their voice in praise freely given to the Creator."[113]

The *Catechism* might have said this about the Incarnate Word, Jesus of Nazareth. It is eminently true of Him. For He "is not only the Word of the Father to us; he is also the perfect response" for us to the Father.[114] Everything He says and does shows God's glory in creation.

The *Catechism*, however, does not say this about Jesus. It says it about each one of us. It is perfectly true about Jesus and about us, too, because we are made in His image. Our life's purpose is to say yes to the Father's creating and then to respond by imitating Him as perfectly as we can.

This is why we are asking: what do we know about Jesus' human experience of God? What did He sense and feel about the all-holy One? What was His perspective on human limits and His perception of evil in the world? What did He ask God for?

We might hesitate to ask such intimate questions, not only about One who lived a while back, but especially about One who is far above us. But Jesus kept none of it secret. He said and did many things that revealed His experience of God. Some were public, as when He prayed out loud before His disciples. Some were private, as when He went off to pray alone.

From experience, Jesus was inclined to urge His disciples to pray by *shutting themselves up* alone with God. Jesus had experienced the

Father *in that secret place*, the context of which is being alone. But Jesus' startling phrase that your Father *is in that secret place*, is not geography. The "place" is available to each of us, all the time. St. Catherine of Siena, a doctor of the church, explained that there is a little room in each one's heart where only they and God can go.

Jesus also told them that, when they pray in public, they should not *babble as the gentiles do*. He saw this as more than a matter of manners. In His view, that kind of *babble* is an insult to God. It's using God. It suggests not really believing that *Your Father knows what you need before you ask him*.

Yet, when He told them, *Pray then in this way*, He included a lot of asking in it:

> Our Father in heaven, hallowed be your name. Your kingdom come. Your will be done on earth as it is in heaven. Give us this day our daily bread. And forgive us our debts as we also have forgiven our debtors. And do not bring us to the time of trial but rescue us from the evil one.[115]

This was His own prayer—we call it the Lord's Prayer—and it tells us a lot about Jesus' thoughts and feelings about God. He starts with *Our*—a prayer for the community, in solidarity with the people. Some leaders insisted, saying more than they knew; *We have one father, God himself.*[116] Jesus grew up believing that. He always addressed God as Father, from the time he called the Temple "my Father's house" to His dying words, *"Father, into your hands I commend my spirit."*[117]

Calling God "our Father" did not mean what the People seem sometimes to have felt: that they owned God. We need to notice this. God far transcends life on earth. When Jesus prays, *"Hallowed be Your Name,"* He is asking for a "democratic" grace: that all the people on earth abandon their little gods and hold His Name uniquely in reverence. His People did this and had long prayed that all peoples would:

Let the people praise you, Lord, let all the people praise you.[118] Jesus was praying with the People.

Jesus had to ask that grace even for the people He grew up among in His "Galilee of the Gentiles." As its name suggests, it was a country where plenty of gods were called on.[119] Jesus' prayer, *Thy kingdom come*, then, was asking a grace for His own People and for all humankind. He thought that big. One time he burst out to His closest friends: *I came to bring fire to the earth, and how I wish it were blazing already!*[120] Not just to Galilee and Judea—*to the earth!*

But Jesus had to be patient because how that fire spreads is up to the Father. All times and events are. So, Jesus could not promise James and John to sit at His right hand and His left, because *it is for those for whom it has been prepared by my Father.*[121]

Jesus had a deeply personal experience of the Father's dominion. He often said that there were things that He *must* do, clearly because God had ordained them, and they were simply to be done. Jesus lived with this mystery, most confident of the Father's care.

Though Jesus' experience was that this mighty God *governs the nations on earth*, He also experienced the injustice and wretchedness that people around Him inflicted on one another. He had, Himself, to pray God would move in power to save us. Jesus loved the earth and loved humankind. His prayer was never that God help us escape this earth. Rather: *Thy will be done in earth, as it is in heaven.*

If we did God's will on earth, we would live in unshakeable peace and joy even when surrounded by evils. Jesus was convinced of this while He suffered various evils.

One evil He experienced was hunger. There was no food security in Jesus' place and time. In Galilee, there were no tall granaries—Galileans could only dream about storing food for security. Many, perhaps almost all, who farmed were tenants. The owner could well be the king, but whoever it was took what he wanted of the harvest. The people lived on what was left to them.

That became a tight issue once Jesus had begun traveling around. He had to depend on hospitality even for His daily meal. The evening meal was the main nourishment of the day. So, when Jesus prayed, *Give us this day our daily bread*, He was not using a metaphor to ask God for a good life. Jesus was asking for supper. And He was going among the impoverished.

Jesus loved the Temple and its prayers and sacrifices, but maybe he loved best people who were down the social ladder. He considered the sacrifices excessive and misdirected. He resonated with the vehement dictum that Isaiah put in the Father's mouth: God has *had enough of burnt offerings of rams and the fat of fed beasts*. What God wanted was a people who *cease to do evil, learn to do good; seek justice, rescue the oppressed, defend the orphan, plead for the widow.*[122]

But the People kept sinning and praying, *Have mercy on me, O God, according to your great mercy.*[123] Jesus was expressing a prayer common in His time: *forgive us our trespasses.* But He went far beyond what was common in His time (or any other) because He felt intimately that God forgives us *as we forgive them that trespass against us.* That was His last petition to the Father as he was being nailed to the cross.

Jesus' own prayer included asking the Father not to test us. *And lead us not into temptation and deliver us from evil.* Jesus prayed that, yet He would experience evil raw and powerful—it destroyed His flesh in the end—and he had to ask the Father for deliverance, trusting. And the Father did deliver Him, in an unexpected and magnificent way.

When we feel we are being tested, we need to remember that the Father will deliver us as He did His Son.

For Consideration

- Note how entirely Jesus trusted the Father in His prayer.
- I wonder which part of the Lord's Prayer speaks most loudly in my spirit.

8

The Tradition of "The Gathering In"
Luke 6

Context and Condition

During Jesus' lifetime, most of the People lived in exile. Perhaps four of every five Jews lived in other countries, not in the Holy Land. More Jews lived in Egyptian Alexandria, for instance, than in Jerusalem.

They lived in the "diaspora," the result of repeated scatterings of the People from the Holy Land. This was not as it was meant to be: God had intended them to flourish in their own land. But Ezekiel had warned them that they had provoked their own exile. By ignoring the Law and willfully serving other gods, they had destroyed "God's People" from within and so had defiled the Holy Land. So, acting through the gentiles, God scattered them to foreign lands.

The readings in synagogue told the stories of these scatterings, which went on repeatedly for five hundred years. Joseph and Jesus heard these heavy memories read from the holy books—Deuteronomy, Jeremiah, Haggai—during synagogue worship.

They also heard that God had promised that He would once again gather His People, Himself. *Do not fear, for I am with you; I will bring your offspring from the east, and from the west I will gather you; I will say to the north, "Give them up" and to the south, "Do not withhold."*[124]

This "Gathering in" was a great hope in Jesus' day. Not soon, though. In common belief, this was to happen at the *end of days*, in a great cataclysm and upheaval. Then, God *will set up over them one shepherd*, a branch from King David.[125]

As Jesus matured, he came to see Himself as this promised shepherd. In His eyes, the crowds around Him were *harassed and helpless, like sheep without a shepherd,* aimless hungry people.[126] Eventually, Jesus will tell His friends: *I am the good shepherd. I know my sheep and mine know me.*[127] Jesus was beginning the "gathering in," in what seemed like ordinary time. If there was any cataclysm, it was in people's hearts and families, in the way the People lived together.

We know now that Jesus was establishing the permanent Reign of God on earth. It was so gradual that the People did not connect it with the end time, and even His disciples had a hard time understanding what he was doing. After Jesus had risen and was about to ascend to the Father, *when they had come together,* they still asked Him, *"Lord, is this the time when you will restore the kingdom to Israel?"*[128]

They were still looking for the great shake-up. But Jesus had started a "gathering in" at the Jordan, when he spent a whole afternoon with a couple of men who had followed Him and asked where He lived. He yearned to know His sheep and to invite them to know Him.

Then Jesus moved to Capernaum. As His ministry continued, He called a few to stay with Him, and He would explain to them what the crowd would not be able to understand.

Fairly quickly, Jesus shaped a core, starting with two sets of brothers in the fishing community at Capernaum. He grew very close to them, often staying in Peter's house and using it as a gathering place. They quickly became known as "His followers."

This was the beginning of God's gathering in. It was humble and, as a presence in the Roman Empire, invisible. We know now that it was God, indeed, who was "gathering in, who is the Shepherd of His

People—and humankind's king and Savior. And as Jesus had prophesized in a parable, people have *come from the east and the west and from the north and the south and sit down at the feast in the Kingdom of God.*"[129]

The "feast," like the One who gathers it, is humble and known only to those who believe. But we believe that there will be an end to time when the City of God is definitively established, surrounded by a great wall founded on twelve foundation stones: Jesus' apostles.

But the Reign had a humble beginning as Jesus brought divine love to earth, gathering His disciples and friends.

Consideration: Jesus Experiences Gathering the Twelve

Now it happened in those days that he went onto the mountain, and he spent the whole night in prayer to God.[130] Jesus often spent the whole night on this rise outside the city. This night, His prayer prepared a decision. Jesus discerned that the time had come for Him to take a concrete step in the promised *gathering in.*

Jesus had learned as He grew up that *the Lord your God has scattered you*—scattered the People among the pagans. Jesus also learned that wherever they were, they resolutely remained a people of their land. The great hope alive among them now had been expressed by the prophet Ezekiel: *You shall live in the land that I gave to your ancestors; and you shall be my people, and I will be your God.*[131] Land, People, and their God went together. And this *gathering in* is what the People in Jesus' day were looking forward to, a little like the way we now look forward to "going to heaven." As God had led them out of Egypt, so God would bring back the exiles *out of all the lands where he had driven them.*[132]

Jesus had come to see that it was His purpose to start the gathering in. Before He had been long in His ministry, He could count on seventy-two to work with Him. His heart was so great, He had yearned for many, many more. But they didn't come. Later, He will look over the city of Jerusalem and feel deeply grieved. His friends will watch Him weep in sorrowful frustration.[133] He will exclaim that he had yearned *to gather your children together the way a hen gathers her chicks under her wings*—so tenderly, and they would not let Him.[134]

He had found, though, many who remained loyal to Him, some of them devoted disciples. But He had learned over time that the way disciples followed Him depended on the gifts the Father had given them. Lazarus, Martha, and Mary, for instance, stayed home. There was Mary of Magdala and Nathaniel from Bethsaida, who were with Him a lot. There was generous little Zacchaeus, still in his mansion, and the upright Joseph of Arimathea. Most were to stay where they were, living as the Father had given them to live.

Most happily, there were His fishermen friends on the lake and several women. Jesus had found those who would stay with Him as He went all over Israel, not knowing where they would lay their heads or who would give them their daily bread. When He had told Peter and Andrew, *Follow me*, He meant that they were to be *fishing for people* the way He had been.

And they did; they went with Him, doing whatever His Spirit guided Him to do. They were a wonderful gift to Him, and He cherished them. Peter and Andrew, along with James and John, had *followed him* as He had gone *around the whole of Galilee*.[135] He grew close to them as they became His most intimate male friends.

They had witnessed the growing conflicts with lawyers and Zealots who were attached to the benefits their hard-earned learning brought them. Jesus' appreciation of the Law was different from their own and made scribes and Pharisees question and criticize Him, and some grew convinced that He was a devil.[136] His close disciples watched those tensions develop.

But this night, He set those tensions aside as He prayed. He discerned that the time had ripened. As Jesus saw it, the Father had already prepared for His choice *those whom you took from the world to give me.*[137] By now, He knew the close ones well enough: Peter, loyal without measure, insightful enough, but impetuous to a fault. Jesus felt how Andrew stood in his big brother's shadow.[138] He knew Simon—*the Zealot*—was deeply attached to the Law and maybe to armed rebellion as well; and James, son of Alphaeus, devoted tightly to the People. Matthew knew the world of wealth. And then there was Judas Iscariot—puzzling, but Jesus knew He was to choose him.

He needed twelve. For when the Lord *gathers the outcasts of Israel, heals the brokenhearted, and binds up their wounds*[139]—the Twelve *will sit on twelve thrones judging the twelve tribes of Israel.*[140] So when it was daytime and they came to find Him, *he called his disciples and chose from them twelve, whom he named apostles.*[141]

Now they were Twelve accepting to be *fishers of men,* not to stay on these shores forever, but to be sent to the ends of the world. So *He named them apostles,* a common Greek word saying *sent* and pointing to a purposeful, undefined future.

Down in Judea at the Jordan, Jesus had asked Andrew and another, *What do you want?* They had wanted, it turned out, to be with Him.[142] And he knew that some others wanted to stay with Him, too, so He had drawn Philip from Bethsaida and the fishermen brothers, James and John. He had promised them a different mind and heart than *how it was said to our ancestors.* And they had truly begun to understand His Good News of redeeming love.[143] He will gladly say to the Father: "*I have given them the teaching you gave to me and*—this was deeply gratifying to Jesus—*they have indeed accepted it.*"[144]

Jesus lived always aware of His own challenge *to cast fire upon the earth* and at times, the feeling rose keenly in His heart: *would that it were already kindled!*[145]

On this dawning day, though, with His friends on their hill, before going back down to the crowds, Jesus knew that He had done what His Father wanted. With His friends, His heart was content.

For Consideration

- Can I believe that Jesus made a fallible human choice of those he wanted close to Him?
- I consider that Jesus' heart is quiet and content to have me with Him.

9

The People's Greatest Religious Genius
Luke 4

Context and Condition

We are asking a great grace: *to know more clearly the human experience of our Redeemer.* That human experience included some knowledge that we must consider supernatural knowledge—after all, some very human mystics have had plenty. But if we set any supernatural knowledge aside, we have to recognize that Jesus of Nazareth was a religious genius.

What is a genius? Well, look at the ones we consider geniuses. No one taught Michelangelo to see David standing inside a great hunk of white marble. No one taught Hildegarde of Bingen to hear "the music of God in all things." No one taught the mediocre nun, Teresa of Avila, how to pray as a mystic and become a doctor of the Church. No one taught Iñigo Lopez de Loyola to find God actively working in everyone he encountered.

They all were geniuses who saw what others didn't see—because God gave it to them to see and appreciate.[146] Jesus saw and grasped the heart of the Law and the full meaning of the prophecies. He appreciated everything that humble obedience to the Father might require. This, especially, had escaped the grasp of the religious leaders surrounding Him.

But geniuses rise out of many others working in their field. Jesus was not a sculptor or musician. His field was humanity's relationship with the Creator. And, just as the geniuses above were people of their own time and place, so was Jesus. They were shaped by the experience of their times: the language, symbols, stories, music, techniques. Geniuses belong in and to their time and place. For genius does not float above the ordinary; it grows out of the ordinary and leavens it from within, as Einstein did science and Shakespeare did language.

And Jesus of Nazareth leavened humankind's relationship with God precisely from within humanity. Jesus did not go to school, though when He was twelve, He had hoped to. Rather, he learned by what scholars call "socialization."[147]

Jesus grew up believing what the People had kept alive of the revelations given by God through the patriarchs and the prophets. Their verbal memory appears to have reached far beyond what we can even imagine. The Word was handed down generation to generation by parents and teachers, helped and urged on by speakers in the synagogue who knew great tracts of what we now have in writing. The covenant at Sinai, the exodus from Egypt, the forty years wandering, the promised land, the infidelities of the People, the promise that *God will be king*—these were things everyone knew in Galilee and Judea.

Jesus' memory was full of these. And we always keep mindful that Jesus' memory was untrammeled by guilt, shame, sloth, or self-doubt. And His self-appreciation was utterly free of vanity, negativity, and binding attachments. Later in Jerusalem, He will say quite plainly about Himself: *As I hear, I judge; and my judgement is just, because I seek to do not my own will but the will of him who sent me.*[148] Jesus had learned as He lived day by day that the Father was shaping Him as the

People's holy Redeemer. Day by day—just as the Father has chosen to form every one of us, His disciples, day by day.

Jesus hit this target that others did not even see: The *musts* that God has planted in our humanness describe the human flourishing and happiness we are made for. Jesus' genius allowed Him to appreciate how we flourish under true authority and how obedience may seem to be self-abdication but, when done with God, is in fact the deepest possible self-affirmation.

This is what Jesus lived to show us. For Jesus came to His genius insights the way Michelangelo came to his: chip by chip, stroke by stroke. And the way Ignatius came to his: examen by examen, discernment by discernment. So do we all.

Consideration: How Jesus Must Go to Other Towns

After He had walked about some of the towns in Galilee, Jesus had settled in Capernaum and made it *his city*. He had walked a lot—driven by the urgency He had seen in John the Baptist. He went all along the lake to Bethsaida, Chorazin, Capernaum, Gennesaret, and Magdala, doing *the work the Father has granted me to accomplish*.[149] And even in sophisticated Capernaum, *his teaching made a deep impression on them because his word carried authority*.[150]

Capernaum was a trading city, important enough to have a garrison of Roman soldiers, which Jesus had not seen in Nazareth. The gentile commander was a centurion—an unusual man *who built our synagogue for us, himself* and who came to believe in Jesus more than most.[151] The little city served as a stop-off on the Via Maris, the great trade route that connected landlocked Damascus to the north with Egypt's ports in the south. Thus, Capernaum had a tax office. Jesus got to know its head, Levi, well enough to call Him as a close collaborator.[152] Levi had a big house and spread out a supper for Jesus and His friends, and some Pharisees, too.

On Sabbath, Jesus regularly taught *in their synagogues*.[153] This was a simple matter of standing up during the service and reciting or reading a passage from the Hebrew scripture—the prophets or the Pentateuch. Hebrew was no longer the people's language, so the speaker would deliver a *midrash*, a paraphrase, interpretation, or what we would call a homily. In the synagogue of flourishing Capernaum, Jesus could find and read scrolls containing the Scriptures.

On other days in Capernaum, Jesus always felt welcomed in the house of Peter and Andrew, which was larger than many. He felt at home in Capernaum in a way He had not been able to feel at home in Nazareth, where He had grown up—not after narrow-minded people drove Him away for telling them the truth about themselves.[154] Capernaum was *his city*—an expression suggesting that Jesus loved living there. But one morning, Jesus was praying and was given a grace that changed things.

> *And when it was day he left the house and made his way to a lonely place. And the people sought him and when they found him, they wanted to keep him from leaving them. But he said to them, "I must preach the good news of the kingdom of God to the other cities also; for I was sent for this purpose." And he continued his proclamation in the synagogues of Judea.*[155]

For the first time that we know of since He used it as a boy of twelve, Jesus uses an expression that He will use at several crucial points in His life: *I must*. The expression names an experience of a chosen value, a fixed purpose, and a choice freely taken—all in one experience: *I must*. The experience is common enough; every mature person has felt being somehow bound to choose to do something.

It is also profoundly personal, not like a legal imposition, but an obligation, a necessity, that comes from our own hearts. The felt need comes not only from conscience, though that is involved; it's more than moral. Jesus could not ignore this *must* and be true to Himself and to His Father. Whenever He says *must*, Jesus knows that He is to do something because of who He is and who He is to become, and because almighty God is His Father.

But these *musts*, as experienced, are also profoundly social and even political because they are enacted. When any of us does something we *must* do, those around us are necessarily affected; our act becomes part of the irrevocable past for all of us. When Jesus did in great holiness what He *must* do, He was establishing, *at the time appointed by the Father* and in this place, the reign of God critically *among you*. His life-arc, He knew, was the magnet drawing all those *chosen by my Father* into His kingdom. He knew the Baptist was correct: God is now launching His reign, and Jesus is to *gather the outcasts of Israel.*[156]

Yet, His experience is on an ordinary morning in an ordinary little city on a lake. And His social experience on this morning is not unusual: a popular, wonderful person has to leave and is being cajoled by the people not to go. The people were of *his city*, the one He had chosen. His response suggests that it was tempting. *I must preach the good news of the kingdom of God to the other cities also; for I was sent for this purpose.* Clearly, Jesus likes these folks who are cajoling Him. He lets them feel that He's under some pressure, and He explains His reason to them. It is His life purpose.

It is notable that Jesus found in His prayer on this morning that He must go preach in the synagogues of Judea, the southern kingdom. At least some of the leaders there were aware of what He was doing. Some scribes and Pharisees, *hearing all that He was doing*, had come up to Galilee *in great numbers* to see what they would make of Him.[157]

Now He is going to them, with His Galilean accent, to the more sophisticated southern kingdom. He knows only that He is to go there—and on whose authority: *For I have not spoken on my own authority; the Father who sent me has himself given me commandment what to say and what to speak.*[158] And later on, He will, on His own authority, declare that John the Baptist was the promised Elijah *and they did not recognize him, but they did to him whatever they pleased,* and beheaded him. *So also the Son of Man is about to suffer at their hands.*[159]

Jesus' genius is something like a perfectly tuned Stradivarius violin. From it comes only perfectly accurate and deeply realized notes. And from Jesus' mind and heart and hands come enactments splendidly conformed to the will of the Father. Every one of His experiences—great or small, joyous or sorrowful, pleasant or painful—reveals how the human can be one with the divine.

Jesus knows this, from experience and from graced knowledge. For now, disappointing a lot of people in His city of Capernaum, He quietly leaves to do what He *must do—continue his proclamation in the synagogues of Judea.*[160]

For Consideration

- Through prayer, Jesus interpreted His *musts* as the Father meant them.
- Can I name some *musts* that are common in our culture, felt by all of us? What is good in them?

10

Jesus Reveals the Heart of The Law
Luke 7

Context and Condition

As we ponder the human experiences of the Redeemer, we realize that the Incarnation gives us a very different God than anyone ever imagined, a God who is closer than close, having experiences in our own human flesh.

We are considering that the Incarnation does not end with Jesus in the Lady Mary's womb. It emerges in the definitive, profound transmutation of sin-broken humanity—the bearer of God's glory in the cosmos. The Incarnation does not present us just an infant in a manger; it presents us with a new human existence.

For our Redeemer remains in our human flesh, tenderly changing once and for all the meaning of human existence. Even wounded by our sin, He loves us with a love we recognize. And He keeps the marks of the wounds we inflicted on Him, changed to glory—showing us that our own wounds do not condemn us but, because of His mercy, will accompany us into glory.

Jesus earned His human experiences as He grew lifelong in *wisdom, age, and grace* and through His death. Early on, He chose to have the experience of being baptized among us who need to be cleansed of guilt and sin. He chose to experience the burden of hurting others by making mistakes. He chose to have coworkers who faltered and tested Him—and He even chose to experience rejection and abandonment by those He had come to love and to save.

So, we are learning that Jesus did not come to save souls. He came to save people—even those who were afraid to accept His redemption. With them, He was patient and persistent. Here we are remembering that Simon the Pharisee was notable among them.

Simon the Pharisee was important enough that people in Galilee remembered his name, though most Pharisees that Jesus encountered remain anonymous. For men like him, conforming to Greco-Roman customs was repulsive. So, it's quite ironic that the banquet Simon invited Jesus to was just such a pagan custom. As we have seen, the customs of the Assyrians, Babylonians, and Greeks endured in the Holy Land during the centuries after their invasions. The pagan customs they introduced caused bitter and violent conflict during the centuries, and Jesus had to discern which of them He could live with.

One of those customs was the lavish dinner with its long conversation and occasional entertainments (like Herod's daughter's dancing). Jesus went to more than one of them. They were in the evening, and doors were open to the curious and the envious. The guests did not sit on the ground to eat as on ordinary days but lay on couches. The point of the banquet was conversation—entertaining, engaging, and long, so that serious topics could be handled seriously. While eating with their hands, guests wiped them on bread (the crumbs for the dogs). The public was welcome, and it seems that occasionally a prostitute would come looking for clients, for the profession was active in the Holy Land. The Pharisee who gave this banquet clearly believed that the woman wiping Jesus' feet was one of them.

We are told that Jesus went to many of these banquets, valuing them as places for formal discussion and always hoping to draw the participants to belief. Jesus' perspective on them was different from

His perspective on the Cana feast. For while other guests were enjoying themselves, Jesus was *doing the work the Father sent me to do*. He saw little fruit from His labors, as far as any surviving evidence shows, yet He persevered—one of the firmest traits in His human character and one we can imitate as we carry our own crosses.

Consideration:
A Prophet, a Pharisee, and a Woman with Nard

As Jesus had returned to Galilee through Samaria, he had found the people talking about a new prophet finally coming, or perhaps Elijah coming back.[161] He was aware that some had begun saying that He was that prophet. Though He never said it out loud, Jesus showed that He considered Himself a prophet. So, He said on His last journey to the Temple: *For today and tomorrow and the next day I must go on, since it would not be right for a prophet to die outside Jerusalem.*[162]

Jesus was different from the earlier prophets, though. He was deeply personal and loving; He enjoyed each human life He encountered. He had come from the Father to heal and save human life on this earth—each human life. He cherished His own share in human flesh. He liked having little children around Him. He touched the diseased people whom He healed, one by one. With His own spit, He wiped the eyes of a blind man and with His fingers pushed sound into a deaf man's ears. He had made plenty of wine to keep a wedding party going. And without being asked, He will heal a man of chronic sickness at the pools of Bethesda.

We know now that some four centuries after Malachi, the last prophet, went silent, God raises up two final prophets: John the Baptist and Jesus of Nazareth. The People readily understood John; he talked like prophets they knew well, such as Amos and Jeremiah. But as for Jesus, all during His human life arc, people were trying to figure out this other prophet—Jesus of Nazareth.

One who wanted seriously to know Jesus was a Pharisee named Simon. He was well-placed and secure enough to invite Jesus to a banquet. That way, his doubting colleagues could have a long conversation and Simon could watch. He prepared the couches and assigned the places. A devout man, he would see to it that each guest was given water to wash their hands and a servant to wash their feet.

During the long dinner, a woman known in the town as a sinner—it makes sense to think of her as a courtesan who supplied wealthy men with what they felt they needed—came and began weeping so copiously that her tears were wetting Jesus' feet. He did not recoil even when she let down her hair—which was then a gross public indecency. She began wiping His feet with her hair. Then she broke into a jar of pricey, fragrant ointment and began anointing His feet with it.

Simon feels that he has his answer and thinks to himself: *If this man were a prophet, he would have known who and what kind of woman this is who is touching him—that she is a sinner.*[163] Jesus reads in Simon's face how he is missing the whole point of what the woman is doing. He values Simon's believing in Him; that's why He's here. So rather than cite the Torah about how God has chosen to forgive, Jesus tries to invite Simon to embrace the heart of the Law, which is love, precisely in the triple relationship among Simon, Himself, and the woman who—this really disturbs Simon—*is touching Him!*

Jesus first shows His own relationship to her. Docile to the situation, undisturbed by the woman's touch, even her caress, Jesus recognizes her behavior as rising out of love for Him and joy at His message of mercy. He loves her, enacting His own teaching: *you must set no limits to your love just as your heavenly Father sets none to his.*[164]

And He deals lovingly with Simon, though He perceives clearly that Simon needs to repent of his lovelessness. Jesus tells a story about two debtors, one owing a great deal and the other a little. The creditor forgives them both. Which will love him more? Simon condescends to answer with a shrug: *I suppose the one for whom he cancelled the greater debt.* Jesus agrees that Simon has judged correctly.

Then He draws a parallel between the greater and lesser debtor on the one hand and on the other, the weeping woman accepting Jesus' message of mercy and an upright man who doesn't own his need for any mercy. But Jesus is gentle as he challenges the Pharisee. Turning toward the woman, He says to Simon,

> *Do you see this woman? I entered your house; you gave me no water for my feet, but she has bathed my feet with her tears and dried them with her hair. You gave me no kiss, but from the time I came in she has not stopped kissing my feet. You did not anoint my head with oil, but she has anointed my feet with ointment. Therefore, I tell you, her sins, which were many, have been forgiven; hence she has shown great love. But the one to whom little is forgiven, loves little.*[165]

Jesus is not complaining about His treatment. He is comparing Simon's self-righteousness with the woman's self-abasement. He is not angry with Simon; what would He accomplish with that? He is interpreting Simon's shameful discourtesy for what it is: Simon has *loved little.* Jesus calls attention to Simon's neglect, which shows that he does not respect himself, and then to this disgraced, despised woman's attention, which shows that she loves—Jesus, to begin with, but herself in the end, for *she has shown great love.* Jesus perceives that the Pharisee's uprightness was not even true self-love. Loveless, he could not love this woman who was his neighbor—or Jesus, who was his salvation.

It is still the case. Lovelessness and uprightness for its own sake freeze Pharisees in unbelief. The vice is pride. In her humiliation, this woman believes in and loves Jesus, and the fire of love has melted her loveless sinning into repentance. Accepting mercy, she is freed to holy love.

There is the heart of this prophet's message, if only the honored upright would embrace it. Jesus wishes they would and keep working at it. For now, gladly and sweetly, *he said to her, Your sins are forgiven. Go in peace.*[166]

For Consideration

- What made Jesus think to connect the love this woman was showing Him with her repentance for her sins?
- Receiving the Sacrament of Reconciliation is receiving the infinite love of God whom I have offended. What makes me think that?

11

A Disciple Always Has a Master
Mark 3

Context and Condition

Being a disciple was a well-understood social arrangement in Jesus'
time, and Jesus naturally adopted it. Jesus had thought to be a disciple
with a master, Himself, when He remained in the Temple. His parents, by God's good grace, kept Him from that mistake.

Jesus knew that a disciple asked a master to adopt him. If the master agreed, the disciple stayed with him. The disciple committed himself to obeying the master and adopting the master's opinions about
the Law. He would memorize his master's sayings. The disciple imi-
tated the master's eating habits and his way of talking with others.
Disciples even washed their masters' feet.

This master-disciple relationship became a powerful bond. Disciples revered their teachers, calling them *rabbi*—a word rich in meaning: *master, teacher, revered one*. The disciple remained with his master
until the master chose. Then the master would send his disciple to be,
himself, a master and rabbi.

In this context, Jesus came promptly to be considered a master, a
teacher, a *rabbi*. Followers had been attracted to Him beginning at
Jordan when two of the Baptist's followers called Him *rabbi* and sig-
nificantly asked Him *Where do you live?*[167] Then they spent the rest

of the day together. It did not take very long before Jesus had some thinking of themselves as His disciples: *Lord, teach us to pray, as John taught his disciples.*[168]

Many men and women chose to be followers of Jesus. Once in Capernaum, when there were great crowds around Him, some of them were declaring, *"Teacher, I will follow you wherever you go."*[169] Jesus told them the cost of following Him, but He chose carefully those He invited to be His disciples.

Note that Jesus broke the cultural pattern of discipleship when he told His closest friends: *You did not choose me but I chose you.*[170] (Most of us still have trouble remembering that.) He broke the cultural pattern in another way when He began teaching in synagogue. He was not sharing. He was teaching and instructing, even though he was not known as any master's disciple. And some who had to cite a master as their authority felt personally diminished when people were astounded at Jesus' teaching, for He taught them as one having authority, and not as the scribes.[171]

As master and rabbi, Jesus needed no other authority, and he lived very differently from those who depended on it. He lived hand-to-mouth, begging, and had *nowhere to lay his head.*[172] Those who were His closest disciples learned to do the same. They also had to learn a final way in which he differed from other masters.

Jesus bluntly told His disciples, *I came not to be served, but to serve.* In this culture where honor and shame were urgent, His disciples found that hard to credit, as they show when the time came and He washed their reluctant feet, despite their reluctance to have Him do so.

He was confident enough as a rabbi to tell them *no disciple is greater than the master, but the fully formed disciple is like the master.*[173] But He perceived that He had to show them what He meant. So He served and they were to serve. *But you are not to be called "Rabbi," for you have only one Master and you are all brothers*, and have one Father in heaven. *Nor are you to be called "teacher," for you have one Teacher, the Messiah.*

His purpose with His disciples was to help them accept being like the Master, *the way, the truth, and the life.* We do well to keep in mind that Jesus still wants His disciples to be like the Master. He is doing that now through the work of the Holy Spirit on those *destined to be formed according to the pattern of the Son.*[174]

In the end, Jesus docilely followed the final stroke in the cultural pattern of discipleship. He sent His disciples to go in their turn and do the works the Father gives them to do. They are to be like their Master: *I appointed you to go and bear fruit.*[175]

But there will always be only one Master.

Consideration:
Jesus Gives "The Sermon" from Peter's Fishing Boat

By now, Jesus has already gone about the cities of Galilee and south into Judea. He still has *many things to tell* as he returns to "His city," Capernaum. A crowd quickly gathers, so Jesus goes down to the shore of the sea with His disciples. That doesn't help: a lot of people, *hearing all that He was doing,* quickly gathered. And with them, also *great numbers from Judea, Jerusalem, Idumea, beyond the Jordan, and the region around Tyre and Sidon.*[176]

Jesus has been traveling the area and curing a lot of people. And a lot more are eager to bring their illness or disability to Him for healing. A crowd can become a mob, mindless and destructive. So, *because of the crowd*, Jesus asks Peter and Andrew to bring the boat around so that the crowd will not crush Him.[177]

When this event occurs, He has already named the twelve followers He's chosen as the apostles. He has explained Himself to them, patiently watching as He got them ready to understand more and more fully that, *If any want to become my followers, let them deny them-selves and take up their cross and follow me.*[178] The Twelve and sev-eral women—His mother, Mary of Magdala, Mary the mother of James and Joseph, the women who have followed Him from Galilee and looked after Him—have absolutely left everything to become His disciples.[179]

But He knows many who would not leave everything; they will be ardent followers but not like The Twelve. And there would be many, many others. He thinks how ordinary their lives are to be. He knows he must describe life in the kingdom. Now He wants to tell them how people who have really entered the kingdom of heaven can live—not day to day as He did. What are they like?

But the crowd has become so unruly in its desperation to touch Him that Jesus can't tell anyone anything. So He gets into one of the boats, the one belonging to Simon, and asks him to put out a little way from the shore. The people walk down into the water, barefoot or in sandals—in this arid climate, tunics dry fast. Then Jesus sits down and teaches the crowds from the boat.[180]

They might be just another crowd in His life. But He looks out on them and sees *sheep without a shepherd*, and His heart yearns to shepherd them. He wants to teach them. He wants to give them hope—that's why He came. So, Jesus describes the heartset and mind-set of members of the kingdom. He says many things, and His disci-ples listen and try to remember.

When they thought about this after Jesus had left them to go back to the Father, His disciples would later gather these bits together. It becomes "the sermon." Some will remember it as "on the mount"—the hill that's probably visible from where he sat in a boat, the one they liked to go to. Others will remember it as "on the shore of the lake." One connected it with the time Jesus taught while sitting in Peter's boat, people standing in the shallows all around Him.

What they all remembered, though, was how plainly He talked to them, how He made their minds clear and their hearts burn. He told them what the Father had sent Him to tell: *Blessed are the poor in spirit, the merciful, the pure in heart.* Any who are like that are the happy ones—and already building the kingdom of God.

They are not commonly the warriors, the erudite, the princes. No—God's kingdom is filled with people who are *meek, peacemakers,* and those who *hunger and thirst for uprightness.*[181] Every time someone hurts or harms them, they *forgive the sinner from the heart.* They always forgive one another—*seventy-seven times in a row,* when that is what it takes. They even *forgive their enemies.* Far from demanding an *eye for an eye, they do good to those who hurt them.*

The way God's kingdom works is shown by its turning a cultural principle on its head. The traditional proverb advised "Do not do unto others what you do not want them to do unto you." In God's kingdom, it's "DO *unto others what you want them to do unto you.*"[182] This is the positive operating principle of the pure of heart.

Jesus knew from the start that after He had shown them how He did it, He would give them His own command: *Love one another the way I have loved you.*[183] His disciples remembered that He had called it *his new commandment.* They also remembered that He had said that only after He'd shown them how to do that.

For Consideration

- As He sat in that boat, what was Jesus wanting for the crowd around Him?
- What story do I tell myself about human life and the cosmos? Does my story really begin in Jesus Christ?

12

What Jesus' Parables Tell about Jesus Matthew 13

Context and Condition

Jesus' parables must have been extraordinarily vivid as He told them. They surely were extraordinarily memorable: Parables are a full third of what His disciples remembered and wrote down in the Gospels.

Today we think of parables as making a clear point, illuminating an easily grasped truth. But Jesus was not just illustrating a truth. He told parables to challenge His hearers and to confront them with a choice: believe or take the consequences. He saw that some accepted enlightenment and were enabled to believe the truth; others were confounded and put off.

Jesus saw these differences as part of the situation He came to heal. As far as we know, He didn't speculate on this difference in gifts. He simply watched how some of the crowd, *seeing they do not perceive, and hearing they do not listen, nor do they understand.*[184]

Jesus' disciples became puzzled about why the Master talked to some people in parables instead of just talking plainly. So they asked Him. His answer is what He felt about them, His disciples: *To you it has been given to know the secrets of the kingdom of heaven, but to them it has not been given.*[185] That's all. Such are the Father's gifts. And remember to pray, *I thank You, Father!*

Jesus clearly valued the differing gifts of those who came to take in what He said. He also knew that people responded differently because they brought different gifts—and varied dispositions—to listening. The gifts ranged from minds clear to dim, and from hearts generous to tight. And the dispositions of their hearts were special to each one. Some, Jesus perceived, received the Word the way a dry path receives the sower's seed, others like rocky ground, and others like rich soil.[186] Each came with their own gifts and in their own condition. And Jesus docilely accepted them in their diversity. His perspective on it was that He was to adapt Himself.

He would not adapt the message He brought. But Jesus understood that it was not as easy to take in as a drink of water. He knew it would turn *father against son and daughter against her mother.*[187] Perhaps above all, Jesus understood how confounding it was precisely to the "upright," the serious seeker. They were particularly challenged by His message that the Father's mercy falls on the good and the bad. They had thought that the only worthy ones were the upright, like themselves. Jesus wanted to help all of them listen and believe.

At the same time—this is something we need to see—His parables tell what He felt about Himself and His work, too. He was maturely human, so he was sensitive, docile, and imagined both present and future. He was also reflective and, as we say today, self-aware.

Well, think of what He was feeling when he told these parables. So the kingdom of heaven is hidden like yeast in dough—what was Jesus' perspective on making it known? He saw that weeds would grow along with the wheat; how did He feel as He watched His own revelation crowded out by critics and unbelievers? His sorrow when people wouldn't listen had this double edge: it cut into their belief and unbelief, and it cut into His own joy and sorrow.

As we pray considering all of this, we will once again learn that we cannot enter empathetically into another's experience without throwing light on our own experiences and our own selves. We are doing what Jesus did and then mandated to His disciples: *Take my yoke upon you and learn of me;* as I took up my own yoke to show you how to take up yours.

And Jesus could confidently add to this, from His own experience: *Do not be afraid.*

Consideration: Jesus' Experience as a Sower of Seed

Early in His ministry Jesus saw that stories kept a crowd attentive to what He wanted to tell them. He had heard plenty of stories as he listened to the Torah every Sabbath—the rabbis were great storytellers. So were the workmen in this oral culture. During the years Jesus spent working as *the carpenter's son,* He would have enjoyed the stories Joseph and other craftsmen told to lighten their long workdays.

He had a treasure of stories as he began standing in Synagogue and teaching. Then early on in Nazareth He, too, had a significant experience when he first preached the Good News: the people just didn't get it. Jesus had *marveled at their unbelief,* clearly having expected something different from His proclamation.[188]

He had been a new teacher then, a neophyte. He had discovered that, all too commonly, most people couldn't or didn't hear what He was really saying—that this really was *good news.* Or anyhow, they wouldn't. Jesus quickly learned how much people needed help to open their minds and let the Spirit touch their hearts. He learned to do what the rabbis did: tell stories.

Like all teachers with real ability, Jesus learned a lot about Himself as He taught others. He had to perceive, once He began facing crowds of listeners, that He was not going to accomplish the work that belonged to generations of His disciples. His mission was not an ending; it was a beginning.

His work was to plant the seed. His parable about the sower of seed suggests that this divine Sower is content: He sleeps and rises, night and day, *and the seed sprouts and grows, he knows not how*.[189]But He knows this is the Father's design, and His patience will be rewarded when *the harvest has come*.

Yes, Jesus wanted passionately to spread the fire of love in His heart. This was His mission to the People. He surely had hoped for better responses, especially in the lake cities where He had done many of His powerful works. He had expected the citizens to *repent* of their greed and violence, and to begin living as members of the kingdom. Too many did not.

He was disappointed but did not experience that as personal frustration. His concern was for them: *Woe to you, Corozain* and Bethsaida and Capernaum. They were like the wedding guest who enjoyed the feast but came without a wedding garment. As that negligent guest was, so they will be *cast into the outer darkness*.[190]

This seems a dire thing for Jesus to have said. But He saw that there are dire consequences for not accepting the Father's invitation. They had been foretold. He saw the repentant ones resting *in Abraham's bosom*, and He saw a chasm between them and those who did *not listen to Moses and the prophets*, and who will not *be convinced even if someone rises from the dead*.[191]

Jesus did not give in to frustration (maybe one or other time, briefly) because He knew that the Father's justice is like that of a wealthy man whose guests beg off from his great dinner. He sends servants to find guests anywhere, *that my house may be filled*. And those who beg off? *I tell you, none of those men who were invited shall taste my banquet*.[192]

But God's mercy is not mob rule; he cares for each of His children. Jesus' joy in telling about it radiates from the shepherd who found a sheep that had been lost—happier about that one than about all the rest just now. Just so, *there will be more joy in heaven over one sinner who repents than over ninety-nine righteous persons who need no repentance.*[193]

Jesus kept stumbling over the *ninety-nine righteous who need no repentance.* They seemed to crowd His days. But He knew that He had to begin the *gathering in,* however small the beginnings might seem against the grand future. Jesus accepted that this is what the Father has in mind, because *He has hidden these things from the learned and the clever and revealed them to the little ones*—like those whom He has already gathered: Peter and Levi, Magdalen and Joanna, wife of Herod's steward.[194] These were the little ones who were the beginning of the gathered community of the kingdom. Jesus tenderly called them His *little flock* and told them that "*it is your Father's good pleasure to give you the kingdom.*"[195] So Jesus accepted and rejoiced in it all.

Jesus' parables show that He is entirely at peace with this slow spread of the kingdom: wheat grows daily to harvest, yeast penetrates slowly. As He preaches and watches the varied responses, He comes to see that the Good News has everything to do with ordinary human existence: a treasured coin lost, a crooked manager finagling, fair pay for a day's work in a vineyard.

He loves the earth in all its rhythms and realities, and His experiences emerge in His parables: farming, building, making wine, patching garments, paying taxes—and personal experiences with many saints and sinners. His part of the earth was familiar with flash floods washing out houses of mud brick that, foolishly, were not built on a stone foundation.[196] Jesus lived His conviction that His word was that stone foundation.

Jesus saw that the kingdom of God is, indeed, *hidden* in these ordinary events. It's like a plowman doing the routine work of plowing up a rented field who turns up a bag of money someone had hidden in a hole. When he finds that bag, he goes and sells everything he has and buys that field. Listeners could hear Jesus' joy at the thought of anyone reaching so wholeheartedly for the Reign.

His joy, though, has its best source in the little ones. Even toward the end of His life, He must grieve for the hard hearts among the learned and the powerful. He imagines them like the managers of a vineyard who killed the absent owner's representatives. When the owner sent his own son, *they took him and cast him out of the vineyard and killed him.*[197]

He tells that parable to the Temple priests and the leaders. They know who Jesus is talking about. Themselves! As He tells the parable, He reads understanding in their eyes. So He reminds them of a great parable from the Old Testament:

> *The very stone which the builders rejected*
> *has become the cornerstone;*
> *this was the Lord's doing,*
> *and we marvel at it.*[198]

Jesus, it has become evident, boldly takes that prophecy to Himself. The leaders grow more and more incensed and vengeful.

For Consideration

- What was in His heart when the Lord told about the Sower scattering the seed?
- I think of my favorite parable (Pope Francis loves the Prodigal) and ask: How does it challenge me?

PART THREE

JESUS EXTENDS HIS MISSION TO THE GENTILES

13

Jesus Faced the Needs
and the Noise of Crowds
Matthew 16

Context and Condition

Crowds, and what we call public opinion, formed the context of Jesus' public life. Once He began teaching and healing the sick and the possessed, Jesus spent a lot of time in a crowd. He was promptly surrounded as he began work in Capernaum, for instance: *Jesus went out again beside the lake; the whole crowd gathered around him, and as was his custom, he taught them.*[199] Sometimes the crowds found Him, *they ran ahead of him and waited for him.* But at times, *he called the people to him.*[200]

Jesus quickly learned how to handle crowds: *he again taught them, as was his custom.*[201] He felt glad to face crowds up in Galilee and down in Judea—*he welcomed them, and spoke to them about the kingdom of God.* And He was always ready to *heal those who needed to be cured* because that helped them accept the Good News.[202]

Jesus could remain silent in front of a mob—mindless forces driven to thoughtless action by some spirit, like the one that would free Barabbas. Crowds, Jesus saw as gatherings of persons, feeling each person in a crowd. So He never healed a whole crowd; He healed only one by one.[203] Even when hemmed in on all sides, Jesus could feel the different touches and their meanings. One time when He was shoved and pushed in a crowd, He *felt power going out of him* to heal an individual woman who had a flux of blood.[204]

Jesus developed two problems with crowds. The first grew from the fixed popular opinion that God would send a great king to free the people. A crisis developed somewhere on the coast of the lake when he had multiplied loaves to feed them. Convinced that He *is indeed the prophet who is to come into the world,* they morphed into a mob wanting to make Him king. When Jesus grasped this, He did what He seemed able to do whenever He wanted to: He slipped through a heap of people and *withdrew again to the mountain by himself.*[205]

Jesus' other problem was subtler and developed only gradually. It was commonly believed that Galilee was a hotbed of rebellion. So any leader in Galilee who could command crowds was watched. It seems that at the beginning of His public life, Pharisees and Sadducees had come to find out what He was preaching. But as He began attracting crowds everywhere, even in the Temple in Jerusalem, then they began to be concerned.

Jesus would do a work of power with a crowd around, and *they were filled with awe; and they praised God, who had given such authority to man.*[206] It was that authority the powers feared. The memory of the bloody disorder following the Maccabean Revolt was still vivid in some quarters, a bit like the American memory of our Civil War.

When crowds grew massive—one time, it was *so crowded that they couldn't eat*—then the powers became genuinely anxious about pulling the Roman bullies on their heads. And Jesus, Himself, began warning His followers and disciples about following crowds. *When the crowds were increasing, he began to say, "This generation is an evil generation; it asks for a sign, but no sign will be given to it except the sign of Jonah."*[207]

Then, at least in Jerusalem, the popular opinion of the crowds began to show conflicting feelings towards Jesus. *So there was a division in the crowd because of him.* Some were content to claim: *"This is the prophet Jesus from Nazareth in Galilee."*[208] But popular opinion is notorious. At the great Feast of Tabernacles in Jerusalem, *there was considerable complaining about him among the crowds. While some were saying, "he is a good man," others were saying, "No, he is deceiving the crowd."*[209]

On their own principles, the Sadducees were elitist; they distrusted and looked down on the people as a whole. *But this crowd, which does not know the law—they are accursed.*[210] They were fearful now that the crowds following Jesus could bring the Romans down on them. The crowds were a force of nature and at this juncture, even despots had to deal with them. Herod, for instance, simply wanted to do away with Jesus, but *he feared the crowd, because they regarded him as a prophet.*[211]

We can look ahead now at how the crowds ended. A great crowd welcomed Him into Jerusalem—like King David! Then a crowd, surely not all official, came *with swords and clubs* to the Garden. Next, a crowd, probably selected and organized by His enemies—turned against Him. And Pilate, *wishing to satisfy the crowd, released Barabbas for them.*[212]

However it was to end, Jesus needed to have the People accept Him and follow His Way. And that meant crowds, as the Father wished.

Consideration: Jesus Hears Peter Declare Him the Messiah

A mature man, Jesus came to know His unique relationship with the Father and the Spirit. He was different in some manner from the crowd of humankind. We do not know when He grew to, or was given, perfect clarity about this relationship, but He surely lived a long while aware of it. For instance, He once said openly to a crowd in the Temple for a feast: *"The Son can do nothing on his own, but only what he sees the Father doing; for whatever the Father does, the Son does likewise,"* which suggests an extraordinary relationship.[213]

Jesus kept the Law and the Tradition as it was customarily done, but He enacted it differently from other teachers. When He fasted, for instance, He groomed himself a bit, not wanting to go unkempt as some Pharisees did to call attention to their fasting. Jesus did not need praise to "feel good about Himself."

For Jesus, *the precepts of the Lord are right, rejoicing the heart,* and that was enough.[214] He interpreted the Law not as a frame for each individual's holiness but as a frame for the People's holiness—the holiness of our way of living together under God. So about the wisdom saying, "Do unto others . . ." Jesus remarked: *"this is the law and the prophets."*[215] In Jesus' heart, this is the Law's core: *"You must set no bounds to your love, just as your heavenly Father sets none to his."*[216]

Jesus certainly set no bounds on His love. Yet he was, as we might put it, "His own man." As we've seen, even His enemies admitted that *"you show deference to no one, but teach the way of God in accordance with truth."*[217] He did nothing just for others' approval. For instance, Jesus healed personally, with His own touch; yet He did it in such a way that the healed mute, maimed, and blind praised, not Jesus Himself, but *the God of Israel.*[218]

Jesus praised the God of Israel with them; He heard the word with them and obeyed it with them. He remained always entirely of the People, living the wisest interpretation of their common culture. When He was in a crowd, He was always discerning how He fit into that crowd—the People of God, His people. Jesus experienced how our sin keeps us suffering—and not just the guilty.

The time came, then, when He had to wonder: Are the things prophesized for *my suffering servant* metaphorical spiritual sufferings—the opposition and hatred I am contending with now? Or are they literal physical sufferings? Am I to be *like a lamb that is led to the slaughter?*[219] He prayed and waited; He would do as the Father wished. Those who were closest to Him already knew the truth of what He'd told a crowd: *"If any want to become my followers, let them deny themselves and take up their cross and follow me."*[220]

The Twelve and the women who stayed with Him would have to mix into the crowds of people who came to listen to Him. They would hear people's remarks. They would have a sense of where "popular opinion" was going. Jesus knew that. So as they walked toward the town of Caesarea Philippi—they remembered where this vivid event happened—Jesus asked His disciples, *"Who do people say the Son of Man is?"*[221]

They all had answers: "Some say John the Baptist; others say Elijah; and still others, Jeremiah or one of the prophets." "But what about you?" He asked. "Who do you say I am?" Simon Peter answered, "You are the Messiah, the Son of the living God." This was not a crowd responding, but one stating his own and his close friends' belief.

And Jesus answered Him, *"Blessed are you, Simon son of Jonah! For flesh and blood has not revealed this to you, but my Father in heaven."* Then Jesus told Peter what came with this gift: he was now *the rock I will build my church on.* Jesus now discerns that the Father has given the Twelve the grace to remain with Him in what must come. The crowds still see Him as a wonder-worker or the king to come. But the Father has given the Twelve insight into Jesus' being with the Father. Now, He feels, they are ready to start handling what will happen to Him in Jerusalem.

So as they walk on towards Caesarea Philippi, He begins to explain to His disciples what He has learned in prayer with the prophecies: *He must go to Jerusalem and suffer many things at the hands of the elders, the chief priests and the teachers of the law, and that he must be killed and on the third day be raised to life.*[222]

The first time He said that, the Twelve were stunned. Peter was appalled. Impulsively, he led Jesus off so the two of them could talk. He broke out: *"Never, Lord! This shall never happen to you!"* Then Jesus showed a side of His character that He rarely showed—and only this one time to those He cherished and trusted. He could be thunderously angry. He turned on Peter and said, *"Get behind me, Satan!"* And He accused Him of being what the tradition called *a stumbling block*—an alluring invitation to disobey God.

Jesus tempered His anger and explained the temptation that Peter's care was causing Him and that His own anger was defending Him from: *you are thinking not as God thinks but as humans do.* Peter was following the crowd, believing what was a common opinion: stay away from suffering, never embrace it, it's a curse. Jesus' disciples must learn to recognize the cross where the crowds can see only destruction.

Those who think like the crowd, without God, may "save" their life—for a little while. Those who think as Jesus thinks, with God, will be saved when they see *the Son of Man coming in his kingdom.*[223]

What Jesus gave to Peter and His close friends, He gives to all His disciples: the gift of some understanding of the world's suffering and of finding some purpose in it—and the gift of being crowned with glory as our Redeemer has been. This is not a pious exercise. We are fools if we do not do what is right in the expectation that we will be rewarded. Hoping for reward is not weak-kneed faith. It is the gloss on meek, courageous, well-ordered self-love. Love like Jesus' love.

For Consideration

- Jesus needed to go away from the crowds so He could hear His own heart.
- I wonder whether I have ever followed a crowd away from Jesus.

14

Jesus Responds to Gentiles' Faith
Mark 8

Context and Condition

We've looked at the rich context of the Redeemer's human experience. We've considered His perspective on some things, and how He perceived His lifeworld and those in it. We've considered what He valued and many of His desires, and we have watched Him make decisions.

Jesus had all this experience among the People—His People. We know He felt that He had been sent to the People. He was surprised, or certainly sounded surprised, that a gentile centurion in Capernaum could believe in Him: *I tell you, not even in Israel have I found such faith.*[224] And it seems clear that He had not expected to find it outside Israel. Even after He had been shown faith by the Syrophoenician mother, whose daughter needed healing from *a fever*, He continued dealing differently with gentiles.[225]

Jesus was docile, though, and He learned from encounters in which He was moved by the Spirit to take action. As His ministry developed, He preached to and healed gentiles. Later in His public life, He would tell some of the authorities: *And I, when I am lifted up from the earth, will draw all people to myself.*[226] But He had come to that conviction slowly through experience.

Well, we should feel with Him. Consider how slow we Christians have been to consider ourselves a *chosen race, a royal priesthood, a holy nation, God's own people,* though we've heard about it for two millennia.[227] Not a lot of Christ's disciples today are blessed to have an ancestry among the Jewish people. Most of us descend from what scripture refers to as "gentiles." This is the way things really are.

But at the same time, we need to be courageous about accepting the grace we have been asking for: "to know you more clearly, love you more dearly, and follow you more nearly." For we are still growing, and this spiritual exercise will certainly lead to growth in our image, picture, and idea of the real Jesus of Nazareth.

And it will, at the same time, help us wake up to the truth that we, too, are a chosen people. The conviction is hard to hold on to, scattered and embedded as we are in a secular world. But we are making no mistake when we think of the gentiles in Jesus' life as our ancestors.

They were thoroughly mixed into the People. Once the Twelve Tribes had moved into their ordained territories among the Canaanites, Hittites, and other peoples in their lands, they began intermingling. We're offspring of those other peoples they intermingled with. Praise the God of Israel for his magnanimous love that includes us among his Own People.

Consideration:
Jesus Feeds Four Thousand in the Gentile Decapolis

When they heard that John the Baptist has been executed, Jesus and His disciples left Galilee and Israel *and went by way of Sidon towards the Sea of Galilee, in the region of the Decapolis*—gentile territory.[228] Some of the gentiles were afraid of Him, and some of the Gedarenes will later ask Him to go away. But in this part of gentile territory, crowds followed, *bringing with them the lame, the maimed, the blind, the dumb, and many others, and they put them at his feet, and he healed them.*[229]

As He regularly did, Jesus healed Jew and gentile one by one—*and the crowds were astonished* that the stories they had heard were true, and *they saw the dumb speaking, the maimed whole, the lame walking, and the blind seeing.* But the gentiles in this crowd were not likely to consider Him just a great magician, because He had *taught them* the truth. So *they glorified the God of Israel,* which tells of a beginning of faith.[230]

Jesus has encountered gentiles with faith before this journey into the Decapolis, not long before. He had been walking with His disciples through Samaria from the coast at Tyre, and a Canaanite woman had shouted for His help. He had told them that, *I was sent only to the lost sheep of the house of Israel.*[231] But He had learned from that woman that the Father can grant open eyes and ears to gentiles, and faith, too. Jesus was moved to confirm hers: *woman, great is your faith!* Jesus was fulfilling the prophecy of Isaiah that *the nations will come to your light.*[232] And He healed her daughter.

Now He reaches the lake shore in the gentile Decapolis. When *the large crowd came to him,* Jesus learned that that woman was not the only gentile who believed in Him. As the Father had given faith to the People, so the Father had given faith to many gentiles.[233] So He went on gladly healing and teaching for that whole day and then for another whole day, the people listening to Him and wanting to believe in Him. By the third morning, the people had run out of food and were hungry. Jesus was the first to notice and *called his disciples to him* and told them what He felt. *"I feel sorry for all these people."*[234]

This was the crowd's third day, and Jesus saw that none of them had anything more to eat. He was unwilling to *"send them off hungry, or they might collapse on the way."*[235] His disciples had no solution to the problem, though they still had a few loaves: *Seven, and a few small fish.*

In this scene, Jesus is experiencing the beginnings of other nations' turn to God, a turn that will end when all *the nations will be glad and exult.*[236] He experiences being their shepherd too. So He feels the needs of those the Father has led to this deserted place. He can hardly miss the parallel with one of the People's most vivid memories: the Father feeding the People in the desert with bread from heaven. Now, these are His people? He is their shepherd?

When Jesus tells His apostles, *"I feel sorry for all these people,"* His perspective is the shepherd's. He has a flock in front of Him, hungry to the point of fainting; it is up to Him to serve them.

The Twelve have a different perspective on this situation: it is a clear problem. There is enough money in the bag that Judas keeps to buy a lot of bread. But *"Where in a deserted place could we get sufficient bread for such a large crowd to have enough to eat?"* They have counted: four thousand men, *to say nothing of women and children.*[237]

What Jesus sees is a huge crowd of hungry children, women, and men—never mind how many, just a lot of hungry children whose mothers have no more bread. Jesus' heart is wrung with compassion, and He hungers to feed them. Aware of Himself now as the One sent to begin the gathering in, He begins reevaluating the relationship between Himself and a gentile crowd.

Jesus had not long ago sent the Twelve on a mission to *go nowhere among the gentiles*, but go only *to the lost sheep of the house of Israel.*[238] Now He judges that these gentiles will grasp the meaning of another sign that the Father is reigning among them—even among *them.*

So Jesus decides to do a work of power—a work recalling the People's memory of Moses in the desert and God *raining down bread from heaven.*[239] Jesus decides to take what bread the disciples have for themselves and share it with others. He takes the few loaves and after giving thanks, he breaks them and gives them back to distribute. And then, the fish. *Everyone ate as much as they wanted and there were seven basketsful left over.*[240]

This is what really impressed the Twelve: the numbers, of men and of basketsful left over, as they had on another occasion. And it was surely an exhilarating experience to hand out a few loaves and pieces of fish and not run out. It was natural that they would remember that. Jesus would try to get them to interpret this sign: He was doing what God had done in all the People's history—care for them magnanimously. Jesus will ask them later, maybe with a dash of exasperation: *"Do you still not understand?"*[241]

Well, they didn't. Still. On the record they seem not to have really grasped that Jesus was giving them a sign that the *reign of God is among you.* The Twelve will need the help of the Spirit to grasp that the *gathering-in* is beginning, and God has *pitched his tent among his People.*[242]

It is as the Father wishes. And Jesus must put up with them, compassionately and patiently—He doesn't yet know for how long. So *he sent the crowds away and got into the boat* and went back to Israel.[243]

For Consideration

- How did Jesus' attitude change toward those who did not belong to the house of Israel?
- Similarly, I wonder whether there are "gentiles" in my lifeworld. I consider what signs I see.

15

Jesus vs. a Legion of Spirits
Mark 5

Context and Condition

Jesus grew up in a tradition that believed evil spirits are real. History recorded a few, like the one that vexed Saul, *an evil spirit from the Lord.*[244] Religious leaders around Jesus were not much concerned with evil spirits. When Jesus drove a demon out of a blind and dumb man, some Pharisees casually remarked that *"this man could not throw out demons except by the power of Beelzebub, the ruler of the demons."*[245]

They were trying to destroy Jesus' character in the hearts of those who were wondering out loud, *Could this really be the Son of David?* Jesus could not let them tar Him. With His people around Him in mind, He lacerated His accusers with a blistering argument.

The incident shows that if their leaders were insouciant about spirits, the People as a whole were quite preoccupied with them. And for that reason, Jesus had to be. The crowds felt that spirits oppressed people with sickness, crippled them with paralysis and blindness, confused their minds, and tricked them into idolatry. Spirits lived in cemeteries and came in dreams.

As He matured through seasons of illness and death, Jesus had to discern His beliefs about spirits. He saw spirits actively working in people's bodies and minds and hearts. He saw the evil one as His own opponent. Think of His judgment about Good News falling on a shallow heart: It is like a seed falling *"on a path, the evil one comes and snatches away what was sown in his heart."*[246] Jesus perceived that Satan was *a murderer from the beginning*[247]—the enemy who intends our destruction.[248]

Jesus took the existence of evil as objective fact. But He also experienced spirits moving in His own interior life. We noted that when He saw the hungry crowd, His heart felt *pity* for them—a good spirit. When His friends wept over Lazarus, His spirit was full of sorrow and He wept, too. He felt a tenderness for a widow of Nain who had lost her only son; His Spirit moved Him to tell her, *"Don't cry."*[249] He grieved for the self-satisfied who, in the end, *shall mourn and weep.* After the Twelve returned from their mission exulting, Jesus *was filled with joy by the Holy Spirit.*[250]

He had negative experiences, too. He *was troubled in spirit* about Judas during the Last Supper. When *unclean spirits would fall at his feet,* He showed how repelled He felt by them and sharply rejected their witness.[251]

These were all transient experiences of spirits. But quite often, the spirit that moved Him was consequential. For instance, He was *led by the Spirit out into the desert* and to a turning point in His life.[252] When the time came, Jesus *returned in the power of the Spirit to Galilee* and began His public ministry.[253] And all during the ministry to a people plagued by evil spirits, He felt the evil one opposing Him, often enough through men like the Pharisees, who should have known not to let themselves be used.

We might reflect that these are experiences we all have. In an argument with a good friend, we feel angrily, "Well, you are *wrong.*" Period. A man's distrust of government limits his discernment about vaccination. A mother watches her child win a race and her heart rejoices. And spirits show up when we act: "I was so *glad* to write the check paying off the mortgage." These spirits are interior experiences.

Then, we do well to notice—as Jesus did—that objective evil spirits lurk among us now. We make these spirits our own, sometimes deliberately, more commonly half-automatically. However we share in them, in every case "spirits" contribute importantly to determining how we think and feel and act. And, as Jesus did, we need discernment.

We want to distinguish spirits that lead us toward God, to follow them, from spirits that lead us toward sin, to reject them. We might recall here the pungent remark of one of the church's earliest spiritual directors: *Whoever claims to abide in him ought to live as he lived.*[254] And Jesus lived discerning spirits—never following a bad spirit but spending His days in harmony with the good Spirit.

Consideration: Jesus Was Ready for the Devils in the Pitiful Gedarene Man

By the time Jesus perceived that He faced a whole legion of evil spirits in a pitiful Gedarene man, He had already had a lot of experience with angels and devils. He had experienced the presence and activity of angels and devils all His life. His mother and father had had direct experience with angels. And all the people He grew up among believed many stories about angels and evil spirits.

Though the People of that time lived afraid of evil spirits, Jesus never showed the least fear of them. An evening in Peter's house was typical. People *brought him many who were possessed by devils. he drove out the spirits with a command and cured all who were sick.*[255]

The incident of Jesus addressing the legion in the Gedarene is unusual. It's the only one we know of when He spontaneously addressed an evil spirit, unasked. At times, evil spirits tried to interact with Him, but He brushed them off, rarely giving the spirit any attention beyond His command to go away. Early in His public life, for instance, one tried to defend itself by daring to reveal Jesus' true identity. It called out, *I know who you are—the Holy One of God!* Jesus snapped at it: *Shut up! Come out of him!*[256] Jesus refused to have anything to do with an evil spirit.

That time, and every time, Jesus *cast out the spirits with his word*—nothing more, no calling on the Father or the angels, no incantation, just His word. Jesus' authority astonished people: *he gives orders even to unclean spirits and they obey him!*[257] When unclean spirits left a sufferer, so did the suffering.

For the "spirit" that causes sickness in the body could be one of two kinds. One was an external force, a devil, who was afflicting the body. The other was the person's own "spirit," their *nephesh*—which means their vitality, their life, itself.[258] On one occasion, for instance, some of the Twelve could not cast out a demon possessing a boy. As his father explained, *it seizes him, it dashes him down; and he foams and grinds his teeth and becomes rigid.*[259] It's impossible to tell whether the disciples thought this was an external evil spirit or the boy's own *nephesh*. Maybe they didn't know.

When they brought the boy to Jesus, *the spirit threw the child into convulsions* as the father had explained. Jesus simply commanded the spirit: *Come out of him and never enter him again.* With a screech, the demon left and the boy lay as if dead. Jesus, *taking him by the hand, raised him, and he stood up.* Jesus explained why the disciples could not do what he did: *"This kind can be driven out only by prayer and fasting."*[260] This was His way of saying that they had to live as he lived, utterly trusting the Father—a concrete instance of His being *the way, the truth, and the life.*

It's worth repeating for ourselves what the early disciples made of Jesus' teaching. As we saw, John's first epistle pointed out: *Anyone who claims to abide in him ought to live as he lived.*[261]

Jesus had crossed the Sea of Galilee to an experience with demons among the gentiles. It caused such excitement that the Twelve all remembered the story in great—often conflicting—detail. With the Twelve, Jesus had crossed the sea to the eastern shore, hitting the beach at *the country of the Gerasenes.*[262] They approached a shore near tombs, from which a powerful man, nude and filthy, was watching them. As the boat scraped the shore, Jesus said out loud, *Come out of the man, you unclean spirit!*[263]

When he stepped ashore, the man *ran and worshiped him* and shouted at Jesus, *I adjure you by God, do not torment me.* Some remembered Jesus' unusual move: he asked the demon's name. *Legion; we are many.* Then the evil spirits begged Jesus not to send them away. Let them go into the pigs. So Jesus did; and the pigs promptly *charged down the cliff into the lake, and there they were drowned.* The herdsmen ran to the owners with the weird news about the pigs and the bizarre story quickly spread. People came running to see what had really happened.

The disciples busied themselves cleaning the freed man and finding a tunic to share with Him. Others arrived, harried and excited, and they told what it used to be like for this man's neighbors. They used to try tying Him down but he'd break the ropes.[264] Jesus sat listening to it all. As more and more *came, they saw the demoniac sitting there, properly dressed.* And he was *in his right mind.* The one who was *so fiercely violent that no one dared to pass that way.*[265] And the pigs got the demons. And died.

And before long, *they were afraid.* Not just some of them, but *the entire population was in great fear.*[266] Was this Jesus connected with the spirits? He knew their names! How else could he do this? In the end, *they began to beg Jesus to depart from their neighborhood.*[267]

Jesus is helping not the People who ought to have faith, but pagan unbelievers, some of whom the Father has given faith. With them, he is gentle and compassionate. So when they quakingly ask Him to go away, what he does shows the depths of His character. His disciples later told what they had watched: His meekness, His great authority and power restrained. Without comment, Jesus simply *got back into the boat, crossed the water, and came to his home town.*[268]

One, though, was given faith and was afraid neither of Jesus nor of His power: the freed demoniac. He *begged Jesus that he might be with him.* Yes, he could be, actually—though not in the boat back to Israel. *Go home to your friends, and tell them how much the Lord has done for you, and how he has had mercy on you.*[269] Now, fully self-possessed, this man will be living witness that *salvation comes from Israel.* An ex-demoniac Gedarene will always be one on whom Jesus lavished *liberty to the captive and freedom to the oppressed.*[270]

And this Man of authority and Master of spirits, whatever else He may be, for His disciples He will always be the powerful benefactor who meekly went away from a people who did not want Him among them.

For Consideration

- Think of the complex of spirits moving Jesus as they rowed away from the Gedarenes.
- I ask myself how often I recognize being moved as Jesus was by a spirit.

16

Jesus Gives an Undeniable Sign
John 11

Context and Condition

Of the scribes and Pharisees, Jesus had always wanted two things: First, He wanted them to reach *metanoia*—change their ways of thinking and judging, change their hearts—by accepting the Good News. Second, He wanted them to accept Himself as a prophet sent from God.

Over time, He would want them to see His full identity as Son of God. But He faced men who insisted on more and more proof that Jesus was authentically of God and not a better-than-ordinary wonder-worker. This is the whole business of demanding signs.

We need to note here what we know about signs. A sign is an object, a mark, or an action that conveys a piece of information or an instruction: A red light tells us to STOP; a fever tells us that there's an infection somewhere in our body. We can ignore a sign—not stopping, going to work anyhow—but the sign still confronts us: STOP! Rest and take some pills!

We rarely find it easy to miss the information a sign gives, but we can readily ignore it. When we ignore a sign, it is ordinarily because we are firmly attached to something it threatens. We ignore a stop sign because we are attached to owning the road. We go to work as usual because it's what we're used to. So we pay no attention to the signs.

This "paying attention" is the first moment in any free act. We pay attention to something we are about to choose or reject. Our freedom begins by paying attention. Very young children attend to whatever is around them; we only gradually mature into the freedom to choose what we attend to. And when we refuse to pay attention to something we should attend to, we usually find that we have some attachment that's threatened.

In the case of the learned and upper classes in Jesus' experience, it was clear what that was. They were attached to the wealth, status, and power they got from serving the Temple and the Law. Jesus' "Good News" was that serving the Temple and the Law meant serving the people they were sent to. Remember: *to serve, not to be served.* So they refused to pay attention to Him, and refused even to see the signs that He gave them because their attachments were so fierce.

More and more of them, though, began believing that Jesus was fulfilling not only His promises but the ancient prophecies. As this kept happening, the authorities began to feel that they were facing, not one man, but a movement, and their opposition grew. And as it unfolded, Jesus felt it all the more urgent that His works should be clear signs whose meaning could not be missed. Even the blind man who begged at the Temple gate knew that *it was unheard of that any sinner could give a blind man sight.*[271]

But their meaning could be contested. Their meaning could be distorted by a determined enemy, for instance: He drives them out by Beelzebul. Or, God can't contradict His Law with cures on a Sabbath. And, the little girl was just in a coma. Sadly, we all know from experience how readily we do this.

Jesus sees it clearly. He sometimes shows anger. He feels affronted by self-centered, arrogant men of little talent. But He has empathized with them (we were all reared in this sinful culture), and having tried persuasion and explanation, He discerns that He is to give them a sign that will make them choose: acknowledge the meaning and live the truth, or ignore the meaning and suffer the heinous contradiction in yourselves. Thankfully, this sign will console those who believe in Him and give them courage for what's to come.

Our Redeemer always cared for those the Father had given Him.

Consideration:
Jesus' Experience Raising Lazarus from Death

We know that Jesus went promptly whenever He was asked to come and help. So it was extraordinary that, *though Jesus loved Martha and her sister and Lazarus*, though He knew what Lazarus's illness meant, *he stayed two days longer in the place where he was.* He was across the Jordan from Judea, where people had tried to stone Him.

Jesus has already shown that He has power over sins and the authority to forgive. Now He will do a work of power that will demonstrate his authority and power over death. Jesus knows that Martha would not tell Him, *Lord, he whom you love is ill,* if Lazarus was mildly indisposed.[272] Lazarus is not just sick, as Jesus told the Twelve. *Lazarus is dead.*

He was more than dead; Lazarus was in his tomb. Jesus had held back and not gone to Him *so that the Son of God may be glorified. Glory* had always been given to *the God of Israel* when Jesus did works of power. Before Jesus does this one, He looks up to heaven and thanks the Father for giving Him this work of power so that *they may believe that you sent me.* The glory of this is the Father's, but the Father will lavish it on Jesus. Not for Jesus' sake, but for His disciples' and His enemies' sakes. Martha showed how it worked. When he promised her that *those who believe in me will live,* she said to Him what He wanted to hear: *I believe.* The works of power may have given Him glory, but the glory was not for Him. It was for His disciples—for Martha here, so that she could believe that the God of Israel had *sent me.*

Martha knew Him as her dear friend who often needed supper and a place away from exigent crowds. She knew He needed taking care of—yet she will tell Him *you are the Messiah, the Son of God, the one coming into the world*. Jesus could perceive that, among His closest friends, He has firmly established His claim of a unique relationship with the Creator Lord.

The Pharisees who are against Him are convinced that *he blasphemes*. They recognize His claim, all right—this laboring man with the Galilean accent: he claims to have a special relationship to God Almighty. They have already confronted Him: even *though only a human being, you are making yourself God*. And they shrugged off His response to that.[273]

Now Jesus discerns that it is time to give them the sign that He has promised them: *Just as the Father raises the dead and gives them life, so also the Son gives life to whomsoever He wishes*.[274]

Jesus has done it more than once when the incredulous could hedge the circumstances. The little maid? "She wasn't really dead, she was in a swoon." And who could believe that story from Nain? People tell these stories and exaggerate. So Jesus discerns that now He is to give them a sign that they cannot deny or ignore.

He will give life in a way that no human being can give it: to a man who everyone knows has died—his body washed and anointed, folded in a cerecloth, and interred. And it's been four days now.

Across Jordan, Jesus waits. He is docile. He knows how Mary and Martha will grieve the death of their brother. He knows the crowds will come and stay. But, as much as He loves them, He has discerned that He *must* wait over across Jordan. So He stays for two further days, aware of what is happening with His friends. He waits. The Father has a work for Him to do, but it is days away. Now He must wait.

Finally, on the third day, He said, *Let's go to him*, to Lazarus, to Bethany.[275] He confused the Twelve and the women with Him. He has waited, they thought, because He knows that He is a hunted man. The powerful have Him on a death list.

Jesus had frustrated the powerful too many times. When he blasphemed in the Temple, they were ready to stone Him despite the crowd—right in the middle of the crowd. But He got them to argue and undercut the force of their claim, and they could not stone Him then. They had tried to arrest Him—for once they got Him before the Sanhedrin, they could manage a legal death. But as He had done before, He managed the crowd and slipped off with His friends.

Now His friends are here across Jordan, and they are hunted too. They feel confounded that He now wants to go to Bethany, surely mobbed by the rich and powerful come to lament with the sisters. They stutter. Then Thomas combines bravado, irony, and maybe humor and says, well, *Let's go back to die with him.*[276] So they begin the perilous two days' walk to get to Bethany.

Jesus has a clear perspective on this whole event: He is to do a work of power so clear and pressing that His own disciples will be solidly confirmed in their faith in Him. It will be a sign so great that *many will believe in him* who had not before. Jesus can see, however, that the sign He will perform will corner those in power. They are there in Bethany—Lazarus and his sisters are high in Jerusalem society.

Lazarus has waited too, in his tomb. And when Jesus gets there, He bursts into tears—the kind of weeping that rises from a well of deep sorrow and pain. The sisters chide Him, and he accepts their chiding, empathizing with their sorrow. He does not need to be shown sorrow; he feels His own sorrow. He had to wait until His friend experienced death before He could help him. And He is experienced and astute enough to wonder what they might do to Lazarus, the living proof of Jesus' more-than-human powers.

With Pharisees and important people watching, Martha and Mary lead Him to the tomb. When the stone is shoved aside, the odor threatens to be deadly. Suddenly, Jesus raises His face and shouts: *Lazarus! Come out!* And Lazarus does. He comes out, shedding the cerecloth. Joy, first, is what Jesus experiences: His friend is alive and glistening, and the fragrance is the spiced oil of the living.

Jesus quietly felt the power given Him, in head and heart and hands. But His creative act leaves Lazarus standing unaided and autonomous again. Jesus feels reverence and a bit of awe as Lazarus comes over to Him, smiling, to worship. And perhaps to embrace.

Some of the unbelieving leaders see and finally believe. Jesus is *the life*. Others go back to the Sanhedrin and plot. He really is *the Way*, but His Way will replace ours. They plan to kill Lazarus too, *since it was on account of him that many of the Jews were deserting and were believing in Jesus.*[277]

And on this account, too, the high priest led the authorities to recognize that they had better kill one man, who seems to be on the way to changing the whole People. It was business. They had to see to it that Jesus *die for the nation*. But Caiaphas was the high priest. So it was prophecy, too: *and not for the nation only, but to gather into one the dispersed children of God.*[278]

So from that day on they planned to put Him to death.

For Consideration

- Explore the experience of Jesus' weeping at the tomb. What do you discover?
- We do well to reflect how we live threatened with death.

17

Jesus Teaches that Being Forgiven Doesn't Hurt
John 8

Context and Condition

When the People in Jesus' day committed a sin, they were not doing something entirely private, going against their own separate consciences. When they sinned, they were defiling self and being unclean, tainting others, and violating the holiness of the Holy Land. They felt that the wrongs among them ought not to be, because the all-holy God intended that they not be and was angered by them. Each felt the guilt of all.

We feel sin no less keenly but quite differently. For us, sin is first of all and almost entirely an individual matter: I violate my conscience, no one else's. This is why we find it hard to grasp the reality of sin-among-us, of social sin. Even if we can see how unevenly we apply freedom and justice to the various races, we have real trouble identifying sin in anything that we do. We see disorder and wrongs and suffering; but they are problems to solve, not sins to absolve. Along with that, we must humbly appreciate that our culture does not afford us a deep experience of the holy. It's like our whole religious life is an intimate English Mass with guitar instead of a solemn Tridentine Mass with incense and organ.

In this, we differ entirely from Jesus' People and from Jesus Himself, who lived with vivid ideas and feelings about what was sacred and
what was profane, what was clean and what was unclean. This sense
evoked the whole "holiness code," or rules and regulations about how
to live. And over the centuries, it elicited an ancient system of sacrifices to atone for sin. Twice a day in the Temple, animals were slaugh-
tered and burned to set the defiled People right with the holy God.
Jesus learned that the priests who administered the system took turns
offering the sacrifices in the Temple.

Jesus was taught that the Temple was the holiest place on earth.
There were degrees of holiness, starting with the Holy Land itself,
given by God to the People. Then the Holy City of Jerusalem. Then,
going up Temple mount: first the Court of the Gentiles, where anyone could go and where a lot of business took place (the national trea-
sury was in the Temple). Then the Court of the Women, then the
Court of Israel (men only), the Court of Priests (priests only) where
the altar of sacrifice stood. Finally, there was the Holy of Holies,
entered once a year by the high priest on the Day of Atonement. In
pagan temples there were two rooms, and the inner room held an
image-statue of the god. In Jerusalem, the inner room was empty,
waiting for the coming of God, of whom no image was possible.

Holy People, holy land, holy city, holy Temple with its terraced
courts, and the Holy of Holies. Jesus shared this sensitivity to the
place. And He went often to the Temple, as the Twelve would continue to do *each day, regularly* after His Ascension.[279] Jesus felt the
Temple's deep holiness and showed His zealous feelings when He
drove the money-changers out of the Court of the Gentiles. *My house
shall be called a house of prayer for all the nations; but you have made it
a den of robbers.*[280]

All these truths about the Temple contribute to the context of an
experience Jesus had there one Feast of Tabernacles. This was the last

great feast of the year, and all males were expected to attend and to bring a tithe of their harvest. In Jesus' day, this feast after the harvests was celebrated as the most important of all feasts.

The city was crowded with people and cattle.

Consideration:
Jesus Refuses to Condemn a Sinner in the Temple

Jesus spent the night before this incident on the Mount of Olives, though He had not intended to be in Jerusalem at all. He had come tardily to the week-long Feast of Tabernacles, which commemorated the tents the People lived in for forty years in the desert. The People's memory was still lively of that event—the Exodus—that had happened hundreds of years ago.

A couple of weeks before His friends left for the feast, Jesus told them that He would not go with them *because my time has not yet come.* And besides, He could not travel around Judea; *the Jews were looking for an opportunity to kill him.*[281] But then His perception of the better thing to do had changed, and he followed His friends, *not publicly but secretly.*[282]

In His prayer on the Mount of Olives, Jesus' spirit urged Him to the Temple. He had gotten only to the Court of the Women when *all the people came to him,* and He generously gave them His attention as they promptly sat around Him. *And he sat down and began to teach them.*[283]

A priest stood at every gate into the Temple, always on guard. Part of his duty was to make sure that no gentile got beyond the courtyard. When Jesus came, in a minute the guardian priest alerted the plotting Pharisees and lawyers. Promptly, they *brought a woman along who,* definitely not clean, *had been caught committing adultery.* They stood her right among the sitting listeners and then announced to Jesus: *Teacher, this woman has been caught in the very act of committing adultery.* There can be no clemency here because *the law Moses com-manded us to stone women of this kind.*[284] It *commands us to stone her.*

They had a perfect case to force Jesus to go against the crowd and lose His power as teacher and leader. The lawyers could tick off the legal points: grave offense (Moses's Commandment on adultery); strict conditions (there must be two witnesses, they must be present and agree); and the Jewish court still has the right to condemn some-one taken in adultery (male or female) to death. This power was being contested because the Romans wanted all life-and-death issues in their own hands. But for now, the Pharisees had the victim, the evidence, and the Law.

Jesus has claimed all along that he does not mean to *abolish the Law.* Well, here is a clear-cut case. The Law *commands us to stone her.* Either He agrees to stoning her or He does not obey the Law. *What do you say about her?* It was not a question but a taunt.

Jesus knows that, in their own minds, they are correct. But He perceives this "case" entirely differently, as He always does. He wants to enact the Good News that God has reconciled Himself to humankind's sins. The Father has chosen: *I will heal their apostasy, I will love them freely; for my anger is turned away from them.*[285] Jesus is proclaiming an *uprightness surpassing that of the scribes and Phar-isees.*[286] Faced with this starkly shamed woman, He cannot shortsight-edly see "a case." He perceives one of God's little ones hurting and sorrowful, and He perceives a flaw in their claims.

Jesus will not debate. He knows He could shame them, one by one—and somehow, He has the knowledge to do it. But He shows no anger toward them; in Jesus' mind and heart, these men are just as burdened by their surrounding culture as this woman is. So He feels compassion for men who have been taught to cherish a dubi-ous uprightness—and also taught to crave the privileges it gives them. *And they love the place of honor at feasts and the best seats in the synagogues.*[287] And they seem to have loved more sensuous things than those: Jesus knows their casuistry—the "two witnesses" must be present at both the sin and the trial. Jesus understands their velvet trap. He'd been tempted in the desert to step into it.

He chooses, instead, to face each one of them with a personal choice that will privately—even in this crowd—confront them with their own need for forgiveness and redemption. He wants to keep trying to help them see what Good News He has brought and how it matters to each of them.

He also feels keenly that this woman is left standing among sitting people, shamed and dishonored by high officials. So when they prod Him, *What do you say about her?* He turns the question back on them and helps them see themselves as he sees them. Go ahead and start the stoning. *Let the one among you who is guiltless be the first to throw a stone at her.* Then He stoops and begins doodling on the floor.

What Jesus did by moving His finger over the dust and dirt on the stone floor, no one seemed to know then and no one knows now—no one, that is, except each of the accusers in turn. Somehow, He was dealing personally with each of these officials. Each of them felt His power and the light Jesus threw on their own consciences and hearts. One by one, they resigned from the jury, *starting with the oldest.*

Then Jesus helped the woman. First, so "the crowd" would be clear that neither "the jury" nor anyone else has passed a verdict: *Has no one condemned you?* And then, with forgiveness in His voice, He said, *Go on out of here,* where you never should have been brought. And He gently let her know that He knew *you won't do this again.*

For Consideration

- Think whether Jesus' dealing with each Pharisee was giving us a model of how God deals with every recalcitrant sinner.
- We need to ask whether we look to one another for glory or are rather concerned with the glory that comes from the One God.

18

Jesus Has Powers beyond Human
John 5

Context and Condition

In His action at the pools of Bethesda, Jesus moved spontaneously to help an abandoned man. That started a whole series of events that tell a lot about the human experience of the Redeemer.

We are asking for the reverent insight into His experience of *the works the Father gave me to do*. What His heart was telling Him as He did them seems to have grown and changed over time. At first, He seemed just to want to heal people and drive devils out of them, and He kept doing it.

But Jesus had a purpose all along: to make it possible for them to believe in the Father's intimate care for each of His children—an intimate care that in this time was the work Jesus was to do. So He was also asking those He healed to believe in Him. *What do you want me to do for you?* was calling for an explicit confession that they believed in Him and His powers.[288]

And it's important to note that Jesus was healing and freeing individual persons. In the past, God had done great miracles for the whole People—bringing them out of Egypt, feeding them in the desert. But Jesus did His acts of power only for individual persons, even when He fed a multitude. He showed by His actions that He valued each person—and wanted that person to believe that God had mercy on their sins and wanted them to live. It also showed that each of us needs to be ready, because *the kingdom of God has come near.*[289] It's now among us.

But as Jesus became known and drew followers, the religious and secular powers grew more anxious, and their opposition grew stronger. Then Jesus clearly began pointing out that His acts of power pointed back to Himself. He once told some Pharisees, *even though you do not believe me, believe the works that I do.*[290] These works showed that He had an authority of His own, under God the Father.

One experience is practically a summary of this development in how he appreciated His power. It happened when He was in Jerusalem and went to Bethesda, the two great pools surrounded by porticoes, and found one of God's little ones.

Consideration: Jesus Healed at the Pool Called Bethesda

On one of His visits to Jerusalem during the festivals, Jesus went to the pools of Bethesda at the edge of Herod's great Temple grounds. Jesus knew that the People believed that these waters, like those of Jordan that healed Naaman the Leper, had more than natural power to heal. Popular belief held that the waters sometimes surged up or rippled. When they did, the first sick person into the water would be healed.

Jesus walked alone—He seems rarely to have been alone except when praying—through the porticoes where the sick waited for the water to be rippled. He found lying there many invalids—blind, lame, and paralyzed.[291] One of them, as was well known, had been lying there *thirty-eight years.*

Jesus looked down at a man who had once been well. He saw that, if this man had been hopeful when he was first put there, his hope vanished over the long years he'd lain there helpless. People now saw merely an old man who had become part of the scenery at the pools.

Jesus saw a man who had no neighbors. He saw a man who had had no help for so long that he had not only lost any real hope of healing but had practically quit wanting to be healed. Jesus saw one of God's little ones whom society has discarded.

This time, he set aside His regular way of asking sufferers what they wanted Him to do for them. This time, he didn't ask. He just saw this very sick man, and His heart led Him to say spontaneously, *Do you want to be well again?*

The man's ambiguous mind and heart shows in his answer. Not a simple "Yes," but a wordy way of hiding how disheartened he is. *Sir, I have no one to put me into the pool when the water is stirred up; and while I am making my way, someone else steps down ahead of me.* And that had gone on for thirty-eight years and left little room for hope.

Jesus decisively commanded: *Stand up, take your mat and walk.* The Redeemer's power gave the man the thought, the desire, and the act. The man felt all at once that he was fine; he knew he could walk, and he wanted to walk again. So, he promptly took up his mat and began to do easily what he had not done for a very long while: he walked.

Jesus moved along among the crowd as the man walked away carrying more than the Law allowed. It was Sabbath. It was in the Temple. There were priests on guard and there ensued a little drama that Jesus had occasioned but didn't witness.

One of the priests stopped the healed man: It is the Sabbath. It is not lawful for you to carry your mat.

The man was full of his exulting experience: *The man who made me well said to me, Take up your mat and walk.* They wanted to know, *Who?* The man didn't know.

The man didn't know Jesus, but Jesus knew him. And Jesus wanted to talk to him again. He had not been teaching there in the porticoes; He had not taken the time to teach the man about repenting and accepting the Good News.

So Jesus found him and confronted him: *Look, you have been made well! Do not sin* any more, so that nothing worse happens to you. Do not live thankless to the Lord for your gifts.

So it was Jesus. The priests who had followed the man to the Temple knew Him. He was breaking the Sabbath, so how could his teaching be true? Jesus knew that they had seen the healed man. He answered them as He had more than once before: *The works the Father gave me to accomplish, these works that I perform testify on my behalf that the Father has sent me.*

But they simply could not get that straight. Their fixed perspective was that they had to make themselves holy by keeping the Law in its minutest details so they could approach God. Jesus' perspective turned that around. He had come to stand among the sinners to be baptized. He came in among his sinful creatures to bring the Good News that the Father had reconciled Himself to them. Jesus was witnessing to the forgiveness of the Father, given freely. And he kept the Law because he loved the Father, who gave the Law. So do we. When we accept that mercy, then we keep the Law, not because it makes us holy but because it is the Father's will and we love the Father. And we discover that his will is finally our glory.

They wanted another human authority—they all had another human authority. So Jesus reminded them that He had John the Baptist behind Him. They had once trusted the authority of John the Baptist, whom they considered *a burning and shining lamp*. They had sent to ask him about Jesus, and John testified to the truth of Jesus' teaching.[292] As to the Sabbath, *My Father still goes on working, and I am at work, too.*[293]

The Father and I working? This is something new. His learned listeners had long been confused; now they are confounded. Jesus has said all along that He is doing the works the Father has given Him—that's one thing. Now He's saying something much heavier, that He is working along with the Father. They were terrified that they knew what He meant—one with God?—this is outrageous—this is blasphemy. And the punishment for blasphemy is death.[294]

They had long been discussing how to destroy Jesus.[295] He had constantly violated the Sabbath and many other plain commandments. Now he was not only breaking the Sabbath, *but was also calling God his own Father, thereby making himself equal to God.*[296] This blasphemy gave them the grounds they had been seeking. They must kill Him.

Then scribes, Pharisees, and Sadducees found themselves working together.

For Consideration

- Jesus did works of power for individuals and for the kingdom too.
- If you had come across a helpless person as Jesus did, how would you have acted as his disciple?

PART FOUR

JESUS OF NAZARETH IS GLORIFIED

19

Jesus Knew His Stature and Its Costs
Luke 9

Context and Condition

Jesus' human experience began as ours begins: bound up in relationships. His were, as He came to know and has told us, rather more extensive than ours.

As we did, the infant Jesus grew aware of others. As his mother nourished Him and drew language from His babbling and then as His father Joseph helped Him learn how to behave and make things, Jesus was no longer just another individual but matured into personhood. As a Person, He thrived in His relationships.

We all become persons as we grow into our relationships. We begin as unique individuals. We grow to be unique *persons*—an indescribably complex creation, tied to and like many other persons, yet not the same. Each person grows from a unique set of relationships, weaving together parents and siblings, cousins and aunts and uncles, coworkers and friends. So did Jesus of Nazareth.

Each of us *knows* our relationships, and only each of us knows the truth of our relationships. That is especially so of the most intimate relationship of all: our unique relationship with our Creator and Lord. This is a relationship we can only barely talk about.

In His unique relationship with Mary and Joseph, Jesus was not just another son of the Promised Land. He was a Person—and by God's grace we believe that He was an even deeper mystery than every other person in the world. We believe what He said about Himself to his special friends: *All things have been delivered to me by my Father; and no one knows the Son except the Father, and no one knows the Father except the Son and any one to whom the Son chooses to reveal him.*[297]

The very human Jesus of Nazareth grew into this knowledge about Himself. In synagogue, the boy Jesus had heard the People's conviction that God's Word was the *reflection of eternal light—a spotless mirror of the working of God, and an image of his goodness.*[298] Jesus was listening to a description of Himself, whom his disciples would come to know as the *visible image of the invisible God.*[299] Jesus of Nazareth is this image, and He said that He is *meek and humble of heart.* We must see that He is revealing something startling about our Creator God. It is an awesome thought that God is *meek and humble.*

As Jesus grew humanly in his personhood, He was enlightened about his relationship with the Father and the Spirit. He was given what theologians call supernatural knowledge as well as supernatural powers. As his disciples grew faith-filled enough to believe what they were seeing, they realized Jesus' holy and supernatural powers. He could tell his most intimate friends about some of his supernatural knowledge, even if they could not really see and understand.

On one occasion, His three most intimate friends could see, clearly and with a brilliance that left them stunned, both His power and His knowledge. He had to admonish them that they should keep this experience to themselves—the three of them—and know that they did not really understand now, but the Spirit would reveal much to them when the time came.

It happened on a mountain, and it reminds us to be docile to the situation about which we do not and will not know everything. We don't live on mountaintops.

Consideration: Jesus Has a Mystical Experience

Jesus stood with Peter, James, and John high on a mountain in northern Galilee. He began to pray. Then he began to shine, emanating a light in which two other figures began to materialize. The disciples were stunned, hovering on the edge of consciousness. They were witnessing prophecies being fulfilled before their eyes.

I will send you the prophet Elijah before the great and terrible day of the Lord—and there was Elijah![300]

And there was Moses, who had promised that God *will raise up for you a prophet like me.*[301] And that prophet was *Jesus!*

The three disciples remembered that they had had to fight to stay awake and did; *they stayed awake*, and they listened to the bright figures talk about *his exodus which he was to accomplish in Jerusalem.*[302]

His exodus refers to Jesus' way of leaving behind a humanity doomed to sin and death and establishing a humanity redeemed and sanctified. For God chose not to redeem humanity from the depths of eternity by striking his creation with one divine edict: *Stop sin! End death!* Rather, God chose something else for his divine glory: humanity, itself, will defeat sin and death. Jesus said something about Himself that ought to be true of every one of us: *God has been glorified in him*, the Son of Man. But then He added something about Himself only: *God will also glorify him in himself* by raising Him alive out of his death by crucifixion.[303] All of this is the *exodus* that Jesus is *to accomplish in Jerusalem.*

Jesus sees this clearly. His triumph is the victory of humanity, itself, over the Evil One. Humankind was caught in a desperate cycle: instead of defeating evil, we were defeating ourselves. Now the man

Jesus of Nazareth comes to defeat sin and death by doing what none of us could do: remain absolutely faithful from birth through death to the Father and the Spirit.

The Evil One has not stopped trying to constrain and trammel our human freedom to love God. In our sinful state, we are easy targets. We are limited in our earthly selves—limited in time and place, limited in physical and spiritual strengths. Our perspectives are limited, our perceptions partial. We deceive ourselves again and again by choosing a thing that is good in itself—an apple, for instance—but one that lies outside the Father's project of our growth in wisdom, age, and grace.

Trying to choose the next good thing, we fall into choosing self-will and end up trying to control our own lives. It's the ancient illusion: *you will be like gods, knowing good and evil.*[304] We do, indeed, *know evil.* From a sad beginning, no man or woman could serve God lifelong in cleanness of heart, *for I was born guilty, a sinner when my mother conceived me.*[305]

Until Jesus of Nazareth. Now, His transformed Self shining on the mountain, the Son of Man is the one who has made the decisive choice against self-will. Lifelong, *I have kept my Father's commandments and abide in his love.*[306] He is learning now what is to come as He, Moses, and Elijah discuss how His *exodus* will unfold in the next hours and days. He is consoled to know that He will still say to whatever comes, *"Not my will, but yours be done."*[307] Jesus is clear about what He would like in His future: *my will.* He loves being among the children of men. His virtues are firm, and He wants keenly to persevere, to keep trying to *do the work the Father gave me to do*—preaching and teaching and healing and giving sight and life.

But it is not to be, He learns as the prophets talk about his *exodus.* How the ex-chief priest will say, *"You do not understand; it is better for one man to die than for the nation to perish."*[308] And how Jesus will indeed die and how the *nation will not perish*—except politically, destroying the leaders. But Jesus will save the People and its mission to be *a light to the nations*. For when *raised up*, Jesus will gather in the gentiles, *that God's salvation may reach the ends of the earth*.[309]

The three on the mountaintop talk about how Judas has decided to take control and make happen what he thinks must. Then the Romans: Pilate will reject doing justice and freeing Jesus. Instead, he will give these despicable men—who are lying and trying to trick a Roman governor—he will give them what they want and trick them: *Jesus of Nazareth King of the Jews*—crucified. And Pilate's brutal soldiers will strip Him and savagely beat the humanity out of Him.

But *because of his obedience*, He will defeat all of it. In this mountaintop light, Jesus feels his victory now and accepts the grace. And for this little while, He glows before his friends, experiencing life in our flesh equal with risen saints. Moses brings with him the number *forty*—years to reach the border of the promised land—now maybe forty hours in a tomb cut into the rock, then forty marvelous days of visiting again those (like Peter, James, and John) who are to go *to the ends of the earth* proclaiming God's glorious victory in our human flesh.[310]

Jesus knows—He's told the Twelve—that the proclaiming will be as laborious for them as it has been for Him. Elijah stands there as the icon of savage enmity and persecution heaped on messengers of real Good News. He had to learn to wait. God's will comes not like an earthquake or a whirling tornado. No. God's victory comes as a little breeze—a little spirit of hope, a little flicker of faith—even in the agonies of an ebbing life.

Now Jesus feels it's time to get on with it. Peter suggests to Him: *"Let's make three shelters,"* stay up here on the mountain, and hold off whatever is coming.[311] *While he was saying this*, a cloud covered them and a voice said, *"This is my Son, my Chosen. Listen to Him."* On the way down, Jesus tenderly reminds them that the other nine will by no means be able to grasp what has happened. Who could explain it? He doesn't mention that the three haven't really understood either, but that's another matter for another time, when the Father sends the Spirit to finish the work of redemption.

Jesus of Nazareth, going down the mountain, knows that his victory, and the victory of the human race, are in the Father's hands. He goes down consoled and confirmed in his decision: *"Father, not my will, but yours be done."* And graced with silent courage.

For Consideration

- Think of the ways Jesus showed courage in facing what He knew beforehand He had to face.
- It is truly sobering to reflect that, because He had chosen us before He began creating us, we are *destined to be molded to the pattern of his Son.*[312]

20

Their Last Evening Together
John 15

Context and Condition

Among ancient peoples, two parties "cut a covenant," perhaps refer-
ring to an object cut in two and to be matched when the agreement
was met. Or perhaps the two parties confirmed their covenant when
each drew blood and they tasted each other's blood. Then they called
on their god, taking their oath in its name. They covenanted; the god
guaranteed.

Jesus believed with His People that, for them, the initiative was
reversed: God took the initiative. God chose Abram, changed his
name, and made him the father of his People. The covenant was
still in blood. It seemed for a while that the blood was to be that of
Abraham's precious son, Isaac. But it was not. To begin with, it was
Abraham's own blood. He and all his male descendants were to be
circumcised, *so that my covenant will be in your flesh as an everlasting
covenant.*[313]

God intended to make Abraham's People a blessing to all the tribes
around his and even to the ends of the earth. Through the centuries, the People were burdened by sin and faltered and they served
other gods. But God remained faithful, sending kings and prophets
to lead them back. And Jesus knew the People's living God, the *God*

of Abraham, Isaac, and Jacob.[314] God was always with them. He, himself, led them.

And then He sent His own Son, a servant king: *I have taken you
by the hand and kept you; I have given you as a covenant to the people,
a light to the nations, to open the eyes that are blind, to bring out the
prisoners from the dungeon, from the prison those who sit in darkness.*[315]
This covenant, too, will be sealed in blood.

We who are Christ's live in this covenant of love. Jesus came into
our flesh as the complete, irreversible expression of God's love for His
human creatures. Now God Himself is in our flesh for an everlasting
covenant. And to be concrete, *I have given you a model to follow, so
that as I have done for you, you should also do.*[316]

Consideration: The Parable of the Vine and Its Branches

In the Upper Room, Jesus has washed the disciples' feet, including
those of the reluctant Peter. Judas has departed, and Jesus knows that
He is now within the reach of the Roman military, who look for trouble during the high holy days. At one point in the long supper, Jesus'
heart is filled with the wonder of their community. He shares his
prayerful insight with them in a rich metaphor: *"I am the vine, you are
the branches . . . and my Father is the vine grower."*[317]

What was in Jesus' mind and heart as He said these things? At
what He knows is their last supper, Jesus feels a oneness among them,
a union beyond what ungraced human nature can attain. Jesus has
prayed for this union among them. He asked the Father *that they may
all be one. As you, Father, are in me and I am in you, may they also be
in us, so that the world may believe that you have sent me.*[318] For He
has been sharing that life with them, steadily more deeply. They have
been open to it, more and more. He yearns to keep them safe in this
new life. *Abide in me as I abide in you.* He speaks as a man to his

intimates, who has given himself to them and has accepted from them the gift of their own lives.

They have worked and rested and walked and talked together. They and He have healed the sick and fed the hungry thousands and freed the possessed. So this *abiding* is not a matter of idea or conviction but of living. It is a matter of enacting the goodness of the believing heart and of witnessing the Good News of God's accepting mercy. *Just as the branch cannot bear fruit by itself unless it abides in the vine, neither can you unless you abide in me.*

Jesus knows at least this about Himself: He has come into humanity from beyond it. He knows that His way of thinking, feeling, and acting harmonize, pitch-perfect, with the way of the God of Israel. He is content that *he and the Father are One* in a way that neither His human language nor any other could describe. He can only feel awe, which does not constrict its object but is an openness to its object's immeasurable reach. Jesus' experience of this harmony is total and permanent—a harmony that His disciples feel but only momently and occasionally. He yearns for us to share it with Him, permanently.

Jesus gives us the means to at least approach this harmony. *You are to love one another the way I have loved you.*[319] This love is the "sap" that runs through the vine on which we have been grafted as children of the Father. It is His love—not something we just feel or believe, but what we do as He did over the course of his earthly life. We are to show it in our own life-arcs. *It is by your love for one another that everyone will know that you are my disciples.*

He yearns to share it with others, concretely with those whom the Father has indicated to Him as His own. He feels consoled that He chose correctly when He chose His twelve, though Judas hurts and grieves Him. So He will later tell the Father in their hearing: *They were yours and you gave them to me.*[320]

Jesus feels that these men and women who have committed themselves entirely to believing in Him now belong to Him and are united
to Him somehow, as He belongs to and is united with the Father. He
values them beyond measure and cherishes their good will—and also
knows their weaknesses. So he points out that the Father will "prune"
his chosen ones of their faults and failings so that they can *bring forth
much fruit, as the Father wishes*.[321] This is the suffering He has foretold. And He knows, after the Transfiguration, how He will Himself
be "pruned." We might reflect that this hasn't changed, either: every
branch that stays is pruned, each of us in our own way. This is the
suffering He foretold.

As the evening ended and it was time to drink the last cup of the
Passover Supper, Jesus decided to inaugurate a process that all can
share, gathering His disciples in a community action that, in symbol
and in truth, will be His way of being *with you all days even to the end
of the age*.[322] He wants us to abide in Him, but He knows from experience that we cannot, of ourselves, achieve that. So He leaves us this
way to honor His invitation to *abide in my love*.[323]

He simply *took some bread . . . and in the same way, with the cup
after supper*, and left in the Eucharist his Personal Presence whenever
we ask Him to come.[324] Now they—and we—know better what He
meant when He had said: *Those who eat my flesh and drink my blood
abide in me, and I in them.*

In a way, Jesus sees this as the "culmination of the mystery of the
Incarnation."[325] God has come into our flesh, uniting to us in our full
humanity. Now Jesus of Nazareth is leaving. But the Son chooses to
be able to come to us "not from above, but from within" the earth's
matter. He comes in a bit of wheat and wine, so that "we might
find him in this world of ours." He remains here, and when we call
Him, He remains at the center of the earth as He is the center of the

cosmos, "the overflowing core of love and of inexhaustible life." This is how He chose to *remain with you all days even to the end.*

So we *abide in his love* because we are built on this foundation. His church is not an idea or an ideal; we are as real as the wheat that made the bread and the liquor of the grapes that made the wine. *For we are what he has made us, created in Christ Jesus for good works, which God prepared beforehand to be our way of life.*[326]

For Consideration

- What experiences made Jesus think of Himself and his friends as a vine and branches?
- When have I felt strongly *belonging?* To what? How? Am I content with that?

21

In the Garden after the Supper
Mark 13

Context and Condition

For nearly four centuries after Jesus' crucifixion, Christians did not use the cross as a symbol of our faith. It was too horrible. And for another thousand years, Christians would never display Jesus dead on his cross. In all that time, theologians were convinced that Jesus suffered in His humanity only. Only the man, not God. They judged suffering an imperfection. So they adopted the notion that God is "impassible"—God could not suffer, being perfect.

Christians who believe that God's love is at work in everything all the time now wonder whether God's love reaches only so far. Perhaps it was easier to believe when suffering was intimate and touched individuals.

It is harder when we watch plagues wipe out millions. What is the Creator doing as millions slowly die of hunger? When rooms full of school children are murdered? World wars. Savage, incompetent dictators. Was God at Auschwitz-Birkenau? Did God watch Hiroshima be obliterated by an atomic bomb? Images of pain and grief, misery and death, are now daily news.

No. We can no longer believe that our God, the source of all being, somehow floats above all the suffering we now witness. Somehow,

God is in our sufferings, and He is sharing His suffering love with us. The mystery of suffering now reaches into God our Lord in His eternity. It is an awesome thought. Somehow, it makes suffering all the more real.

The unbelieving want nothing to do with this mystery. For those without faith in Christ—and we must watch how far we seem to be with them in this—suffering is a problem, not a mystery. For the completely secular person, suffering shows human weakness and lack of control. We can end it, they tenderly believe, if we move in strength and determination. Anyone who knows human history knows how fatuous a belief that is.

Our faith is clear and supported by history and reality. And the church is entwined in this history and reality, as the Council declared: "That the earthly and the heavenly city penetrate each other is a fact accessible to faith alone; it remains a mystery of human history, which sin will keep in great disarray until the splendor of God's sons, is fully revealed."[327]

We are correct to hate suffering. We are surely sensible to avoid and ameliorate it. But we suffer, all of us, and will suffer. And we are among the unbelieving if we doubt that God is with us in our suffering. More powerfully still: we must believe that God is with us as who God is: meek and humble love.

This is what Jesus' passion and death reveal. On the cross, Jesus offers up the self He had developed as the shepherd of the People. In any human terms, He has failed. His sheep are scattered—the few sheep He has. His bare hope is the Father's love.

All the while, the Father's heart is in agony for his Son, joined by the Spirit mothering forth the life that is simultaneously being savagely destroyed.

We understand why Christians did not use the cross publicly for centuries, and why they hesitated for centuries more to show Jesus on his cross. They could not let themselves—we still can't—picture the Redeemer a naked man dying on a cross.[328] He is always modestly wrapped, sometimes with gold. That, itself, is a grotesque failure. And now we face a failure behind that one. We still default imagining the Almighty God suffering. It is a fearful thought.

I have prayed for decades about what brought Jesus to do this. The only answer I have ever had that leaves me close to content is this: Jesus said, *"I wanted to be with you; I had to be with you."* This is how love works. This is how the author of the Letter to Hebrews understood it: *For the high priest we have is not incapable of feeling our weaknesses with us, but has been put to the test in exactly the same way as we ourselves, apart from sin.*[329]

Consideration: Jesus' Experience in the Garden

Here's His context: They want Him dead, the Sanhedrin. One of them has convinced them with the argument: *it is better for you that one man should die instead of the people, so that the whole nation may not perish.*[330] Their idea is that the rabbi from Nazareth will die as a substitute for the People—even those who are rejecting Him feel that. A later generation will see that the powerful priests are blind to the irony of it—how they are bringing the prophecies to fulfillment. *The punishment reconciling us fell on him and we have been healed by his bruises.*[331]

The city is filled with Roman soldiers who don't care one way or another about this Galilean. Pilate is a high-functioning narcissist who seems to have no principles except to defend his position and make sure people know he is important. His attitude will bring him to his end when he's called back to Rome and disappears from history. Meanwhile, he's imposing himself on the Jews.

We can watch how Jesus handles what He knows about all of this. He has led the Twelve to their place in the Garden where they always go. The disciples are sleepy after the long evening and a full meal with plenty of wine. Jesus is not sleepy.

He is aware that they are coming for Him. He has chosen not to escape this time; this is something He must do. His loyalty to the Father, his whole being in and for the Father, require Him to accept what is to come. Jesus knows what the powers intend—He has friends among them who certainly warn Him, as they have done before when they told Him not to come back from the safety he had sought in the desert across Jordan. The Jews will not stone Him; the Romans would allow that but the crowds who follow Him would not. The Sanhedrin leaders intend to maneuver the Romans into crucifying Him, and then the blame will be on Rome and they will be rid of Him.

Jesus knows what they intend. He knows Judas is in it. He feels terror rising in His throat and on His skin. He stands and nods to Peter, and the three follow Him. He needs His closest friends to pray with Him in His hollow fear and feelings of terror. He needs them. But sleep overcomes them.

Jesus views this whole sequence of events—decisions made by men who hate Him, fear Him, or are just indifferent to Him—as His Father's will. That's first for Jesus: it is the Father's will. *Your will be done.* They would have no power over Him *were it not given them.* He has done what he could do and what they would allow Him to do. *"I have spoken openly: ask them,"* he will say.[332]

Now he sees that His death is somehow the Father's way of destroying the evil among the People, and even among all humankind to whom He has come from the Creator's throne. Jesus' body will writhe, and his blood *will be poured at the foot of the altar,* now his cross.[333]

As the high priest said, He is the One being offered from among sinful humankind. He is the Servant of Yahweh. For this, He has come. It is as the Father wishes.

Jesus' docility allows Him to see how the Father loves Him. The Father is love. Yet, because God is like a woman in labor bringing forth all of creation, the Father hands Jesus over to his rebellious creatures to be tortured and crucified—His Father's heart all the while suffering bitterly for His Son. And the Son accepts being handed over, all the while suffering bitterly in Himself and for the pain in His Father's heart. Somehow, the Spirit of Love has come upon flesh, upon the creation that the Father is bringing forth, and now in death's agony.

Now Jesus perceives the real meaning of the psalms and Isaiah and Jeremiah. He sees the duplicity of Judas. Lines of the psalms and of Isaiah run through his mind. He grows aware that He is terrified. Terror seizes Him, a paralyzing fear that freezes His mind in what is to come. Irrational, but He sinks into it, still master of His purposes. It makes Him perspire, heavily, His perspiration turns brown, awash in the oil in His hair and the ointments on His skin. The three whom he has brought with Him *faint* (not quite the same as *fall asleep*).

This he deeply values: *I, if I am lifted up will draw all to my self.* He cannot now think that this is something He has decided: it is the Father at work, slowly but irresistibly, in and through Him. He knows that in a while, He will hear the mob that greeted Him so riotously when he rode in change their song. The crowd that the authorities gather will yell, *"His blood be upon us and upon our children."*[334] Even in His agony, He knows that that is what He wants.

What He wants in this minute is to pray. He wants His closest friends with Him—praying with Him. He wants not to do His own will but the Father's. But He wants to be let out of this ordeal; He does not want to suffer, to be destroyed as a man, and to be cast out of the People. He wants to draw all humankind to Himself. But He wants to do the Father's will. His own will is to stay and heal and teach.

But His purpose this evening is *to lay down his life.*[335] This is what He wants to do. They are not taking it from Him against his will. He could escape and has done so many times before. This time He will not escape because His desire is to lay down His human life entirely freely, giving it—as His enemies have seen—to save the People, though his salvation transcends the political "salvation" the Sanhedrin envisions. Jesus wants His blood to reach them, too, though.

Jesus sinks into fear and terror. He prays because He must cement His will to the Father's. He must find the courage to do what He must do one more time. Then He feels the desire that these men who are destroying Him not be destroyed themselves—*Father, forgive them.* This is His decision when He rises.

They come. He faces them. *I am he.*[336] And He commands them to *let these go* who are not ready yet to join Him in his holocaust. He knows that, with the Spirit, in time to come, they will be.

For Consideration

- Jesus faces physical torture, rejection by his religious leaders, repudiation by the crowd, cancelling as a Jew, and death. Which of these is hardest to empathize with?
- I ask myself, have I suffered seriously and yet kept aware that Jesus is with me?

22

Attending to the Resurrection
Matthew 28

Context and Condition

For as long as anyone can remember, all our Roman Catholic churches have displayed above the altar the bare broken body of the Redeemer on his cross. Church regulations require it, explaining that the crucifix "calls to mind for the faithful the saving Passion of the Lord."[337]

What it doesn't call to mind is the saving Resurrection of the Lord in glory. Perhaps his coming among us in the Eucharist is meant to do that. But omitting the risen Lord from the images that we live with suggests that our own resurrection is a sort of add-on to our faith. It's nothing special to think about—like an icon of St. Whoever on a schoolroom wall.

Even if we do not think about it much, we know perfectly well that our resurrection is not an add-on. The triumphant end of the Creed trumpets it: " . . . the resurrection of the body and life everlasting." Since we do believe in such an astounding fate, you might expect that we'd pray about it in our *lectio divina* at least at Easter season.

We don't. The Easter narratives do not mention "the eternal happiness of the disciples' own resurrection," as Gerhard Lohfink puts it.[338] There's a good explanation why the Twelve and their earliest followers did not look forward to the Resurrection. They expected Jesus to return promptly *in glory* and went daily to the Temple to be there when he came again.

Well, except for a very few of us, we do not daily anticipate Jesus' Second Coming. But that doesn't explain why even mature disciples pay so little attention to the "reward" that Jesus promised to *you blessed of my Father*.[339] He certainly mentioned this glorious reward often enough. His parables often have endings like the promise *to have treasure in heaven*.[340] In one typical parable, for instance, a good king tells his good servants: *"Come, you that are blessed by my Father, inherit the kingdom prepared for you from the foundation of the world."*[341] He explained that those who have left everything to follow Him *will receive a hundred fold and will inherit eternal life*.[342] He widened the promise: *Whoever believes in the Son has eternal life*.[343] Eternal life is the believer's destiny.

Whatever keeps us from living mindful of Jesus' promises, we have one basic reason we want to look forward to our own resurrection: Jesus did. And He has given us a model.[344] Throughout his life, Jesus lived aware of the glory waiting for Him at the end. It was the Father's will, the last of *the works the Father gave me to do*. Remember: when He said He *must suffer*, He added that He *must rise* as well. He lived expecting *the Son of Man to be glorified* in the end.[345] We who have asked to know Him more clearly have this good reason to live mindful of our reward: *Whoever claims to abide in him ought to live as he lived*, and He lived aware of His glorious reward.[346]

The Kingdom of God is among us: we're it.[347] And in the end, we are not going anywhere else. Jesus rose in flesh that belongs to this earth and he has promised to come back to this earth. *"When the Son of Man comes in his glory, and all the angels with him, then he will sit on the throne of his glory."*[348] That is the end time.

If we live unaware of this, we have fallen into the trap that Paul warned the Corinthians about: *If for this life only we have hoped in Christ, we are of all people the most pitiable.*[349] To escape being among those *most pitiable*, a good place to start is considering how Jesus experienced rising again into His own life on earth.

Consideration: Jesus Rises Alive from Death

We have only a few stories about what Jesus experienced when he woke after being dead. We can know, though, that He saw and heard and smelled some things, just by being alive in our flesh. He felt the hard cool of the stone He was lying on, and then the softness of the little cloth He took from His face, folded, and set aside. When the angel *rolled the stone aside and sat on it*, it made some noise, but He didn't hear that. When the women looked inside *to see the place where he lay*, Jesus had already risen and gone.[350]

But we can be certain that He smelled the fragrance of the earth in the morning and was surely thrilled by the splendor of the heavens and the green all around. With a fullness that makes Him radiant, He lives again in the earth that He loves. The harmonies that marvelously link everything with everything sing of an Infinite Creative Benevolence—to us, softly and in phrases. But to Jesus again in our flesh, they sing loudly in the rhythms He loves: sun and shadow, stillness and wind. These are things that Jesus perceived that splendid morning.

Then Jesus began what He woke up to do. He wanted to go to His friends, beginning with the special ones His Father had given Him. He learned something as He did it, we find. Every time Jesus went to His friends, He saw in their eyes that they did not recognize Him. They tended, as we all do, to see not His *Person*, but *an individual* who might have been the gardener or another traveler walking toward Emmaus. We experience this in a diminished way when we look at another and see, not the whole living person, but an individual whom we can categorize and dismiss.

As we sometimes must do, Jesus had to call their attention to the One whom they knew and loved. He might just say aloud their name: "*Mary.*" Or when they're too astounded, He might have to ask, *Have you anything here to eat?*[351] Then they knew Him.

Iñigo de Loyola pointed out in his *Spiritual Exercises* what is obvious once we think about it: the newly alive Jesus would choose to go first to his mother.[352] The Lady Mary knew He would come, though that knowledge surely did little to soothe the piercing grief of her waiting for Him—a grief that He knew His own sufferings had caused. She suffered, harboring in her heart what she surely knew about Him but may not have grasped fully.

Jesus' identification with the Father and the Spirit was a mystery to her, of course, as it was and will forever be to every human creature—a truth simply too big for us to take in, surround with wisdom, and manage. But He was Her son and her cherished joy.

She *knew* from the time of His conception that He would unravel human experience; He would draw from the smoldering ruinous fire of human passions a perpetual blinding light of love and life. She knew that great truth; the particulars, she had had to learn as He did, day by day. Now on *the third day* it comes to one fulfillment. He suddenly stood before her in that new light—exulting, gleaming with human joy to show her how precious she is to Him. Jesus, our Redeemer, showing to her what every child forever owes every mother.

During this beautiful morning, Jesus then went to the other women who had enriched His life and ministry. As far as we know, he let Mary of Magdala be the first to touch—actually, *to cling to*—Him.[353] The other women recognized Him and were thrilled with His promise fulfilled. Then he gave them the mission of herding the Eleven up to Galilee—*there they will see me.*[354]

We know why He valued these women: they loved Him and let Him love them—the value transcending all other values. It may also be that He understood that the men would plow around and break into new frontiers to plant the seed. But in time, it's the women who harbor, nourish, and shape new human life, not the men. He had learned to talk and to behave principally from the Lady Mary while Joseph was off at work. The boy went to synagogue with His father already believing in God and knowing the basics of how to love the Lord.

Jesus' risen experience allowed Him to go where He chose and to be with those He had chosen. With them, He had walked and talked. Now, in His risen life, He freely goes where he wants to be without any kind of "going" that we know about, even if there are large spaces or a locked door in between.

He also plainly valued this time among His friends and still loved long talks and what we would call a party—like a breakfast on the shore in the dawn. He preached and taught again, sometimes to hundreds gathered; we do not know how or where. His perspective on this teaching was that it was to console rather than to inform. He is living in *communion* with them, wanting them to appreciate themselves as He has appreciated them—a new task for each disciple born and baptized.

But, as He had chosen to lay down His life, so He now chooses to *ascend to my Father and your Father.*[355] He does not say what He said of other big decisions, that He *must* ascend. He chooses to ascend. For though His Resurrection has established His Reign on earth, His experience of a human arc of life is ended. Now He wants His friends to share His mission. As he prayed to the Father: *As you have sent me into the world, so I have sent them into the world.* And He is already praying *for those who through their teaching will come to believe in me*.[356] He is already praying for us and thinking to send the Spirit.

As the firstborn and the mighty ruler who has now *subdued all things to his reign*, He leaves us to share with Him *whatever sufferings he has still to undergo* for the sake of our redemption.[357] He has graciously left to us, His friends, to prepare the kingdom of earth that will finally be a fitting return for the Gift given by the Father.

For Consideration

- How did Jesus experience the joy he brought when he appeared to His friends?
- What would I experience if I met Jesus one morning?

23

He Made as Though
He Would Go On
Luke 24

Context and Condition

The village of Emmaus—the place of one of Jesus of Nazareth's last earthly experiences—has disappeared. All we know is that it was a seven-mile walk from the Upper Room, which gave Cleopas and his companion—and then Jesus—plenty of time to talk. But *Emmaus*, the name of an historical village that no longer exists, reminds us of a history that we cannot allow ever to disappear: the inside story of the human experience of Jesus of Nazareth.

For on the walk to Emmaus, two things are going on. First, the Son is looking back over His personal experiences among God's Chosen People and the gentiles. He patiently interprets how He fulfilled *all the prophets*. He shows His companions what He valued and chose in His life's arc. And then He enacts this fulfillment as he breaks the bread. In Jesus' perspective on His last walk on earth *going about all the towns, he is still doing the works the Father gave him to do.*

That is the other thing happening on the way to Emmaus. It is still what He is doing—and He is closing down His work in the kingdom of earth. He spent forty days preparing His friends for His departure and for the Spirit's arrival to arm them for the things to come.

The *things to come* immediately is the church, the communion of believers, the community of faithful. What the Spirit will lead them and us to is *the way they will know you are My disciples*—that is, the fulfillment of Jesus' command *to love one another the way I loved you.* We are now the church. Jesus really wanted to keep us from forgetting who we are: the People of God, his Mystical Body—most visibly, the Community of the Faithful.

Jesus is helping His disciples reflect on the reality that every community gathers a group of people for some purpose. Every great human community (tribe, nation, association, church, sect) has a history, longer or shorter. Its members know its history and interpret their current experience in the light of that history—some, of course, more deeply than others. They live loyal to the community, to its purpose, and to one another. The greater and older the community, the more likely members are to interpret their individual lives most basically in terms of membership in that community.[358]

There's more to this. For instance, a community shares, or struggles to share, an interpretation of its history and current experience. And a live community has some projects in hand. But for the moment, focus on the need for a history that remains alive in the members' memory and gives them an explanation for their experience.

For this is the second thing going on during this amble toward Emmaus. Jesus is making sure that the earliest community of the faithful will keep rooted in this grand salvation history. He is doing it for this discouraged couple, and He will do it for larger groups. And when He has done as well as He can, He will send His Spirit to continue the work. With us, too.

We might reflect that when I declare that I am "putting God first," I mean that I think of myself first of all as Christ's, chosen by His Father to belong to the people who are His elect. After I affirm that, I might be *male or female, Jew or Greek, slave or free*—it won't make any essential difference because, in His Mystical Body, we are equals, we all belong to Him, we are all one.[359]

How we are to live as one is a gritty matter. We do well to ponder Jesus' experiences getting our Community of Faithful established. In this, too, he has left us a model.

Consideration: The Risen Jesus Walks to Emmaus with Two Disciples

The couple abandoned the community in the Upper Room to walk dejectedly, sharing the bitter aftertaste of lost hope. They had believed Jesus to be the *Son of God* and had expected the rest of Psalm 2 to be promptly granted Him: *I will make the nations your heritage, and the ends of the earth your possession.* Maybe they should have known better when He came into the city *riding on a donkey.*

They looked up from their grief to see another walking with them. It was Jesus, *but their eyes were kept from recognizing him.*[360] Of course: they were just grieving over images of His death and burial. They didn't recognize His voice, either, when He asked quietly, *"What are you discussing with each other as you walk along?"*

His question stopped them; *they stood still, their faces downcast.* Jesus felt how full they were of hot memories and emotions—ready to burst—all of them about His recent experiences. They blurted out that he must be *the only visitor to Jerusalem who does not know the things that have happened there in these days.* This is quite an ironic statement—because Jesus was *the only visitor to Jerusalem who really knew all the things that happened there.* But that did not fix Him in a cloud of grief.

He let them go on. *But we had hoped that he was the one to redeem Israel.* And on. *Today is the third day*—and they rattled on about the women and the angels and Peter and John. *Some of those who were with us went to the tomb and found it just as the women had said.* But of course, *they did not see him.*

They meant that they did not see *his body.* None of them—not even Mary of Magdala—imagined Him alive again. They were preoccupied with, *Where's the body?* Everyone knew stories about the dead rising, and everyone knew that believers would rise again—in the far, far future. As for right now, He was really dead.

Jesus felt how the two were walking away from hope, Isaiah's prophecy flickering in their experience: *We turned our backs on him and looked the other way when he went by.*[361] But the risen Lord knew in His heart how numbed they were, unable to wake from a wretched dream, watching the soldiers *divide My clothes among themselves and throw dice for My garments.*[362] He knew, He could feel it, that it had broken their hearts.

He felt tender compassion for them, but He would not want his sufferings to erode the faith they had put in Him. He decided that He could bring them back to themselves by reminding them of the People's—this duo's own—long history of hope. *"Oh, how foolish you are, and how slow of heart to believe all that the prophets have declared!"* Jesus was exulting that his life mirrored the prophecies of a thousand years. *So beginning with Moses and all the prophets,* Jesus interpreted the couple's own experience in terms of his human experience.

He was filled now with power and glory. But He had begun as *a meek and humble* king over a kingdom of earth plagued by sin and death. He had been born in *Bethlehem, in the land of Judah,* which the prophet honored because *out of you will come a ruler who will be the shepherd of my people Israel.*[363] His father Joseph had made Him his own son by exercising a father's right—and also doing what the angel had commanded him to do: *you are to name him Jesus.*[364] Then He was taken to live in Nazareth, *for the boy shall be a nazarite to God from birth to the day of his death.*[365]

When the time was right, he had left Nazareth to go to the desert with His cousin John. There, He had learned that He was not to live as John lived. He'd been sent to the *anawim*, the lamentable remnant, and *anointed to bring good news to the poor*, and freedom to the oppressed, and sight to the blind.[366] He had done all of that.

His voice rang with joy as He remembered that He had gone to all the towns of Galilee and down into Judaea and up to Jerusalem, not to castigate and condemn, but to heal and raise and save. *Yet the peoples saw and did not understand*, and it had grieved Him when *their hearts were hardened*. But He was given to understand *that God's grace and mercy are with his elect, and that he watches over his holy ones*.[367]

He had been sent with God's faithful word to His disloyal People: *you are precious in my eyes and honored, and I love you*.[368] Jesus knew that every one of His words and signs had shown that. But even among the chosen, disloyalty had not ended: *Even my close friend in whom I trusted, who ate my bread, has lifted his heel against me*.[369] But Jesus had forgiven him, and if the hurt endured, Jesus rejoiced that the Father's infinite love and mercy would extend to every sinner.

But that would come later. Back then, the ugliness followed. He had had to listen as *false witnesses come forward against me*.[370] He had been despised and *turned over to the torturers*. But He had submitted. *He never opened his mouth, like a lamb led to slaughter*.[371]

Then, as this pair knew, the soldiers had *pierced his hands and his feet*. Jesus saw them wince, remembering His hideously broken body when Pilate let them take Him down from the cross. They had anointed and wrapped Him properly, cloth on face, and put His body in Joseph of Arimathea's unused tomb. As the prophet had said: *he was put in a rich man's grave*.[372]

Of course, the grave was not the final prophecy. But it was evening, and they were suddenly in Emmaus. *Jesus walked ahead as if he were going on*. But they wouldn't let Him go. Meekly, he ate with them.

Then He showed them what His purpose had been all along the journey. *He took bread, blessed and broke it; their eyes were opened, and they recognized him.* It was Jesus! He had done *the work the Father gave him to do*—and then He was gone.

They hurried back to the Upper Room and told how *our hearts were burning within us while he was talking to us on the road.* Suddenly, Jesus was with them there, too. And once again *He was opening the scriptures for them,* taking the whole roomful of them through their own roles in the People's history so they would realize who they are called to be and never again forget who they are.[373]

This is what He had come back to do.

For Consideration

- What did Jesus make of the hurts and terrible injuries done Him in His lifetime?
- How can I look back over my own life as Jesus was looking back over His?

24

Together for a Last Time
John 21

Context and Condition

As Jesus left His disciples and his friends, ascending to *my Father and your Father, to my God and your God*, they remembered that He had commissioned them to go *do the work the Father gave me to do.*[374] They remembered a good deal more than that as they went about spreading His Good News with tremendous energy. As some of them remembered it, the newly filled Twelve *gave their testimony to the resurrection of the Lord Jesus with great power.*[375]

They had no books and notes to rely on—only the pondered memories of their own experiences with the Redeemer. And they did this amazingly swiftly throughout the Mediterranean world, especially after the Romans destroyed the Temple in 70. Before the Gospel of Matthew was finished, there were so many disciples in Rome that Paul could write to them among those *who are called to belong to Jesus Christ.*[376] Before the Gospel of John summarized the theology of the Word, Peter wrote his first letter to *a chosen race, a royal priesthood, a holy nation*, interpreting for the gentiles Jesus' gift that *you were not a people, but now you are God's people.*[377]

Long before the Gospel of John pondered the experience of the Word among us, Christians were interpreting how *great grace was*

upon them all. For the gentiles, Paul wrote in his first letter to the
Corinthians: *Do you not realize that you are the temple of God and the
Spirit of God dwells in you?*[378] False gods were in their old temples;
they were, themselves, temples of the true God. And starting in
Antioch, they were Christians—made on the model left by the Son
of God. The Colossians may already have been singing a liturgical
hymn: *He is the image of the unseen God / the first-born of all
creation.*[379]

From very early days, though, disciples wanted to know about
Jesus' human experiences: what He said and what He did, how He
saw things and what He wanted. They were not amateur theologians;
they were journaling their own experiences of the Redeemer in
response to His human experiences. They were not speculating like
the Greeks and the Egyptians. Their recollections had a very practical
purpose. From the very start, disciples have known what we've
thought about more than once: *Anyone who claims to abide in him
ought to live as he lived.*[380]

So they kept the stories and wrote them down. They wrote down
a great deal about Jesus' *exodus* in suffering, about the four days of
Wednesday to Saturday in Passover. They wrote much more about
His suffering—perhaps because they were, themselves, suffering
under Nero and his ilk—than they did about the 40 days after His
resurrection.

Happily, we learn from them some things about Jesus' human
experiences during the days after his resurrection. He sought out people. He consoled them. He made sure they knew He had forgiven
them. He gathered them again. And He could be where He wanted
to be, no obstacles, and with whom He wanted to be, who didn't at
first recognize Him. He could eat with friends. He talked about what
had been closest to His heart all His life: *He spoke to them about the
Kingdom.*[381]

One long story they remembered recounted the morning Jesus had arranged to meet His disciples on the shore at Capernaum. What had He in mind about being in Galilee? What was His perspective on this gathering? And when He sat on the shore and watched His disciples pull in empty nets, what was He seeing?

We've learned to ask what He was valuing here, His purpose in gathering them—the fire and the fish, the men and the women. The chance to confirm His love? Or their love? And what in all of this did He desire most? As we know well by now, we will learn by watching what He decided to do.

Consideration: Breakfast on the Seashore

The context is one of the final earthly human experiences of the Redeemer. This gathering of the Eleven is unique in one respect: we know that the women organized it because Jesus had asked them to. And we know that He had looked forward to it since the day He rose. They are back in Galilee, on the shore near Capernaum, *his city*. Jesus is where He loved to be, and His friends are there.

Actually, they are on the lake fishing—Peter's idea, not Jesus' idea or the women's—but one Jesus has adjusted to docilely and rather creatively. Jesus watches them trawling toward the shore of the lake as the dawn breaks. He is enjoying a day different from the day He rose. On that splendid day, they couldn't believe Him; now, they just won't recognize Him.

On that first day, He had found Peter, after leaving His mother. He had looked for Mary Magdalene in the garden and talked to her and to some other faithful women. And then, *on that very same day*, he had walked with the couple to Emmaus. Then in the evening, He had gone for the first time to the Upper Room. The apostles were there, *the doors of the house were locked for fear of the Jews*. Yet He chose suddenly to stand among them. *"Peace be with you."* His voice was not enough; He had to show them His wounded hands and His side, too. They were so wrapped up in marveling and doubting that they were, well, *dumbfounded*.[382]

Jesus saw that they were simply stunned. Who had ever heard of anything like this? With the doors all locked, a dead man is suddenly standing in the middle of them, touching and taking their hands. Jesus saw that His own sheep needed a sign. So now he's asking, *Have you anything here to eat?* Ah. Oh. Yes. Fish. The grilled fish. And *Jesus took it and ate it as they watched*.[383] He simply ate, like a guest who came late to supper. So now they were back to the ordinary. The mystification lessened as He chewed. They could see that He was real, beginning with that first day.

Jesus had chosen to be real in many other contexts, too, in the days between that first day and this last one on the beach. Years later, living witnesses could remember that he had given attention and care to a lot of his scattered disciples, and could tell exactly how long he had stayed around. *After his suffering he presented himself alive to them by many convincing proofs, appearing to them over the course of forty days and speaking about the kingdom of God*.[384] Always speaking about the kingdom of God.

It is clear, though, that from the time He rose, Jesus had intended to gather His closest friends the way He had gathered them many times before—off by themselves to be together. The first word spoken by the risen Redeemer was her name to Magdalene. *Mary!* And then, an angel told the women who went to the tomb, *"Go and tell his disciples and Peter"* to go to Galilee because *"he is going ahead of you."*[385] No need to detail where: *his* city, Peter's house.

So the Eleven went and waited. And waited. Finally, still his impulsive self, Simon Peter said to them, *I am going fishing*.[386] They followed him into the boat.

They trawled all night long and caught nothing. Coming back toward shore as it began to be light, they saw a man standing on the beach: Jesus, enjoying the sight of them as they were when He first got to know them. He asked—empathy in His voice—*"Haven't you caught anything, friends?"* When they all said "No," he stepped in with hope: *"Cast to starboard and you'll get some."* They did, and the net was so full that they could hardly get it in the boat.

John looked up from what was in the net and said to Peter, *"It's the Lord!"* Long echoes of the beginning of things, when Jesus had done this same thing and Peter was so afraid of the marvel that he wanted Jesus out of his life. Not now. Peter wanted Jesus in his life. So he grabbed his tunic *and sprang into the sea.*

When he waded up from the water, he saw *a charcoal fire there, with fish on it, and bread.* The rest brought the boat in and beached it. They saw Jesus and they knew from His habitual way that He was hungry to be with them one more time. He had found wood and fish, had built a fire, and had been waiting for them. Then, *Jesus said to them, "Come and have breakfast."*

He is a good host and has food ready, but He is also wonderfully sensitive about their community. So He tells them to *"bring some of the fish that you have just caught."* And the breakfast goes on. They were eating together again.

All along, He had had a purpose on this shore. The Teacher, He takes them where they are—anguished over Judas and ashamed a bit about Peter. Peter, himself, felt the bitterest shame. But in this culture, everyone around him felt it, and that diminished his standing. Jesus was careful not to call him his nickname, but by his own name. He asked Peter in front of all of them what He already knew: *"Simon son of John, do you love me more than these?"* Peter hunkered down and answered from his brokenness. *"Yes, Lord; you know that I love you."*

He didn't exactly address the "more than these." Neither did he not answer it. Effectively, he left it to Jesus to decide.

Jesus' heart filled with love for this man, and He asks twice more, tenderly matching the other triplet. To make certain the rest of them grasped what He was doing, Jesus added every time that Peter was *"the shepherd of his flock."* He was named *The Rock* from the start and is still the Rock in Jesus' mind and heart—never mind his triple failure. And as history has proven, this Rock lived Jesus' wish: *The greatest among you is to act as if he were the youngest, the leader as if he were the one who serves.*[387]

Jesus will gather them one more time, in a huge congregation. And He will give them His final wish, the only battle plan He has: *Go and teach all nations and baptize them in the Name of the Father, and the Son, and the Holy Spirit.*

And behold, they did what He said.

For Consideration

- Did Jesus enjoy Himself in these last hours?
- Does it make me happy to think of eternal life?

Endnotes

1. Luke 2:52; John 5:36.

2. Matthew 11:29.

3. John 13:15. Another translation—*For I have set you an example, that you also should do as I have done to you*—implies that the disciples should serve one another even to washing feet.

4. Second Vatican Council, *Dei Verbum, Dogmatic Constitution on Divine Revelation*, paragraph 1.

5. Jn. 11:27.

6. Jn. 10:30.

7. Matthew 11:29; John 13:15.

8. See R.T. France, *The Gospel of Matthew*, The New International Commentary on the New Testament (William B. Eerdmans, Grand Rapids, MI and Cambridge, U.K.: 2007), p. 18. St. Irenaeus believed it had been written in the 60s.

9. Colossians 1:15.

10. 1 John 2:6.

11. Romans 8:29.

12. See, as an example, Creighton University's Bruce J. Molina and Richard L. Rohrbaugh, *Social-Science Commentary on the Synoptic Gospels*, 2nd ed. (Minneapolis: Fortress Press, 2003). The authors at times interpret Jesus' sayings and experiences beyond what their actual methodology validates. Scholars face this difficulty when they apply some other wisdom to the gospels.

13. Elizabeth A. Johnson, CSJ, *Consider Jesus: Waves of Renewal in Christology* (New York: Crossroad, 1993). This sober and insightful study focuses

on "an understanding of Jesus' genuine humanity," which the author thinks depends on "how the question of Jesus' self-image" is addressed (p. 35). This method seems to skip over the clear depiction of Jesus' actual experiences in their context, and how they point to His perspective in this situation, His perception, value, desire, and decision. In brief, it skips over His human *experience* and analyzes His "self."

14. Luke Timothy Johnson, *The Real Jesus: The Misguided Quest for the historical Jesus and the Truth of the Traditional Gospels* (San Francisco: HarperCollins, 1997). Johnson saw that this calls for a method that "enables a community of faith that also experiences the powerful presence of the risen Lord to engage these texts (together with the Torah) in a continuing conversation" (p.174).

15. Gerhard Lohfink, SJ, *Jesus of Nazareth: What He Wanted, Who He Was*, tr. Linda M. Maloney (Collegeville, MN: Liturgical Press, [2011] 2012).

16. Acts 17:28.

17. Luke 19:1.

18. Luke 19:10.

19. Exodus 1:1 and following.

20. See "Monsignor Georges Lemaître," "Originator of the Big Bang Theory," drawn on 10.28.2021 from https://www.catholicscientists.org/idea/monsignor-georges-lemaitre-originator-of-big-bang-theory.

21. *Catechism of the Catholic Church*, para. 302. To the unbelieving, this appears as "evolution," and therefore everything happens by chance.

22. 2 Corinthians 3:18.

23. John 5:26.

24. Colossians 1:15. Most translations say *the firstborn of all creation*, seeming to suggest the conundrum that things are born. This translation interprets the whole phrase at once: Christ is first of all humankind—who are shaped in His pattern or image.

25. Romans 8:29.

26. Ecclesiastes 3:14.

27. Yves Congar, O.P., *Jesus Christ* (New York: Herder and Herder, 1966) 52. Congar treats Jesus' "inspired knowledge"—the supernatural knowing of God—briefly and clearly.

28. Sirach 42:15, 22.

29. Proverbs 8:25.

30. Romans 8:29. The Letter to the Romans was written around the year 56.

31. 1 John 2:6.

32. Matthew 11:29.

33. John 8:29.

34. Deuteronomy 11:11. Small rivers ran through Galilee, and springs were common in that ground.

35. Deuteronomy 11:19.

36. The Torah has three meanings: first, the Pentateuch, the Teaching of Moses; second, the entire Jewish Bible, the "Tanakh"; and third, the Oral Teachings, the traditions handed down generation to generation.

37. Matthew 24:37.

38. Matthew 5:21.

39. There were two other times when the men were required to lead their families to Jerusalem: the Feast of Weeks came fifty days after Passover (hence Pentecost) and the Feast of Booths, at the end of summer.

40. Luke 2:42.

41. Luke 1:15.

42. Luke 2:44.

43. Hebrews 4:15.

44. Luke 2:52.

45. Karl Rahner, SJ, cited in Raymond Brown, S.S., *Jesus: God and Man*, p. 50. Rahner's statement is in the article, "Dogmatic Considerations on Knowledge and Consciousness in Christ" in *Dogmatic vs. Biblical Theology*, ed. Herbert Vorgrimler (Baltimore: Helicon, 1964), 260 (an unavailable text).

46. Exodus 19:5. Peter, whom Jesus considered the Rock, knew this very well. In later years, he wrote the first papal encyclical and declared that promise extended to gentile disciples of Jesus: *You are a chosen race, a royal priesthood, a holy nation, God's own people.* 1 Peter 2:9.

47. Leviticus 20:26.

48. Leviticus 19:12.

49. Leviticus 19:2.

50. Leviticus 19:37.

51. Our own conflicts can alert us to how differently we think about "the people." In our moral and religious thinking, as the third millennium

begins, we do not put the common good first. We tend to think the individual's rights are the more fundamental. We expect to build community by organizing and harmonizing individual gifts and desires. We think that if we collect all the individual "rights" and put them in good order, we create community. But today's divisions and enmities show that it hasn't, and it can't. We must admire how the people in Jesus' time were a real community in which the children had a uniquely personal identity. We have not enjoyed that for many decades.

52. Psalm 1:2.

53. Malachi 3:23. See Mark 6:15. When the Twelve told Jesus what people were saying about him, they said, *Elijah the prophet.* This memory was still vivid, four centuries after the prophecy was made.

54. Matthew 11:14. The prophecy is Malachi 3:1.

55. Isaiah 52:7.

56. Matthew 3:10.

57. Mark 1:4.

58. Matthew 3:13.

59. Matthew 3:17.

60. John 12:47.

61. Congar, *Jesus Christ,* 52.

62. Luke 6:43; Matthew 12:33.

63. Colossians 1:15.

64. Matthew 11:29.

65. John 14:6.

66. Matthew 17:7.

67. John 5:36.

68. Mark 11:10.

69. Psalm 136:24.

70. Luke 3:16.

71. John 10:38.

72. Matthew 4:1. This is the passage with all the citations here.

73. Matthew 4:11.

74. Luke 4:16.

75. Luke 4:21.

76. Matthew 8:20.

77. Matthew 4:15.

78. Matthew 13:33.

79. Matthew 13:31.

80. Matthew 13:24.

81. Isaiah 58:2. The wiser among the Pharisees felt the irony Isaiah injected into this phrase.

82. Isaiah 58:3.

83. Luke 12:57.

84. Luke 5:17.

85. Mark 1:27.

86. Matthew 5:20.

87. Psalm 51:5.

88. Isaiah 66:13.

89. Mark 2:1. This is the passage of the following citations.

90. Matthew 6:15.

91. Matthew 22:16.

92. Romans 12:1.

93. John 2:4. "My dear lady" translates a Greek word that was a polite address to a woman. In this case, it might be something like our saying, "Mother, what do you want. . . .?"

94. Matthew 1:19.

95. John 2:8.

96. John 1:11.

97. John 16:28.

98. Luke 13:23.

99. Luke. 6:38.

100. John 2:11.

101. Hebrews 3:14. Note that we are indeed tested, but no test we will be put to could possibly be greater than the test He was put to.

102. Raymond E. Brown, *An Introduction to New Testament Christology* (New York: Paulist Press, 1994) 72.

103. John 5:19. Jesus added: *Whatever the Father does, the Son does likewise.*

104. Galatians 5:1.

105. Matthew 14:23.

106. Mark 1:35.

107. Luke 6:12.

108. Luke 18:1.

109. R. T. France, *The Gospel of Matthew*, The New International Commentary on the New Testament (Grand Rapids, MI / Cambridge, U.K.: William B. Eerdmans Publishing Company, 2007) 239.

110. Matthew 6:5.

111. Matthew 6:8.

112. Matthew 6:6.

113. *Catechism of the Catholic Church*, para. 264.

114. Bernard Haring, *Free and Faithful in Christ* (New York: Crossroad, 1978) vol. 1, 20.

115. Matthew 6:9.

116. John 8:41.

117. Luke 2:49; 23:46.

118. Psalm 67:3, 6.

119. Worshiping a god means placing it first among purposes and desires and taking on the burdens it imposes on its devotees. Currently, secularist individuals worship profit, physical beauty, success, and the little god Orgasm the Great. And in all of this, we are driven by *passions*. Current American culture has grown so irretrievably rational and pragmatic that we simply ignore the force of passion, which is neither rational nor pragmatic and needs constant control to be both.

120. Luke 12:49.

121. Matthew 20:23.

122. Isaiah 1:16.

123. Psalm 51:1.

124. Isaiah 43:5–7.

125. Ezekiel 34:23.

126. Matthew 9:36.

127. John 10:14.

128. Acts 1:6.

129. Luke 13:29, NJB.

130. Luke 6:12.

131. Ezekiel 36:28.

132. Jeremiah 23:8.

133. Luke 19:41. *"When he drew near and saw the city he wept over it."*

134. Matthew 23:37.

135. Matthew 4:23.

136. Matthew 9:34.

137. John 17:6.

138. Jesus grew closest to Peter, James, and John. Once Andrew sat with them *privately* across from Jerusalem in the garden. Otherwise, Andrew does not join them. Mark 13:3.

139. Psalm 147:3.

140. Matthew 19:28.

141. Luke 6:13.

142. John 1:38.

143. Matthew 5:21.

144. John 17:8.

145. Luke 12:49.

146. "Talented people hit a target others can't hit; geniuses hit a target others can't see." This remark is attributed to the German philosopher Arthur Schopenhauer.

147. See the application of this approach to the gospels in Bruce J. Malina and Richard L. Rohrbaugh, *A Social-Science Commentary on the Synoptic Gospels*, 2nd ed. (Minneapolis: Fortress Press, 2003). Note that this is sociology, anthropology, and cultural history, and the authors consciously exclude applying theology and moral thought. For example: Judas repents, throws the thirty pieces at the chief priests and "Thereupon, as a public sign of his repentance and to redress lost honor, he hangs himself" (p. 135). This is how individuals acted in the honor/shame culture; it does not give an adequate account of how this person acted. He lived in a relationship with Jesus of Nazareth and made a lifelong commitment to Him. Any adequate consideration about this person would have to give an account of Jesus' remark about Judas' fate, explain the theology of prophecies fulfilled, and apply moral judgment to his perfidy and his despair.

148. John 5:30.

149. John 5:36.

150. Luke 4:32.

151. Luke 7:6.

152. Mark 2:14.

153. Luke 4:15.

154. Luke 4:28.

155. Luke 4:42.

156. Psalm 147:2.

157. Mark 3:8.

158. John 12:49.

159. Matthew 17:12.

160. Luke 4:44.

161. Matthew 17:10.

162. Luke 13:33, NJB.

163. Luke 7:39.

164. Matthew 5:48, NJB. Other versions translate Latin's *perfectus* as *perfect*, which in current usage suggests *fixed in itself and needing nothing else*. The Latin actually means *complete, fulfilled, embracing all that pertains to it*.

165. Luke 7:43.

166. Luke 7:49.

167. John 1:38, NJB.

168. Luke 11:1.

169. Matthew 8:18.

170. John 15:16.

171. Mark 1:22.

172. Luke 9:58.

173. Luke 6:40.

174. Romans 8:29.

175. John 15:16.

176. Mark 3:8.

177. Mark 3:9.

178. Matthew 16:24.

179. Matthew 27:55.

180. Luke 5:3.

181. Matthew 5:6.

182. Matthew 7:12.

183. John 13:34.

184. Matthew 13:13.

185. Matthew 13:11.

186. Matthew 13:3.

187. Luke 12:53.

188. Mark 6:6.

189. Mark 4:27.

190. Luke 10:13.

191. Luke 16:31.

192. Luke 14:23.

193. Luke 15:7.

194. Matthew 11:25.

195. Luke 12:32.

196. Luke 6:48.

197. Matthew 21:45.

198. Psalm 118.

199. Mark 2:13.

200. Mark 7:14.

201. Mark 10:1.

202. Luke 9:11.

203. Luke 17:12. Jesus healed ten lepers at once in this unique incident. Only one came back.

204. Mark 5:30.

205. John 6:14.

206. Matthew 9:8.

207. Luke 11:29.

208. Matthew 21:11.

209. John 7:12.

210. John 7:49.

211. Matthew 14:5.

212. Mark 15:15.

213. John 5:17.

214. Psalm 19:8.

215. Proverbs 24:29; Matthew 7:12.

216. Matthew 5:48.

217. Luke 20:21.

218. Matthew 15:31.

219. Isaiah 53:3.

220. Matthew 16:24.

221. Matthew 16:13.

222. Matthew 16:21.

223. Matthew 16:28.

224. Luke 7:9.

225. Mark 7:26.

226. John 12:32.

227. 1 Peter 2:9.

228. Mark 7:31.

229. Matthew 15:30.

230. Matthew 15:31.

231. Matthew 15:25.

232. Isaiah 60:3.

233. In his magisterial study *The Gospel of Matthew*, R. T. France considers "the second feeding miracle is to be interpreted as a Gentile counterpart to the Jewish feeding in 14:13–21." See page 597 and the fuller treatment on pages 599–603, where he will point out Matthew's "deliberate intention to draw a parallel between Jesus' Jewish ministry and his ministry to Gentiles."

234. Matthew 15:32.

235. Matthew 15:32b.

236. Psalm 67:4.

237. Matthew 15:38.

238. Matthew 10:5.

239. Exodus 16:4.

240. Matthew 15:37.

241. Mark 7:18.

242. John1:14.

243. Matthew 15:32.

244. I Samuel 16:14. Remarks like that "*evil spirit from the Lord*" show that their discernment was not always easy.

245. Matthew 12:24.

246. Matthew 13:19.

247. John 8:44. The *Catechism* teaches that Satan "was at first a good angel" and then he and others became evil "by their own doing." *CCC* 391.

248. Luke 10:19.

249. Luke 7:11.

250. Luke 10:21.

251. Mark 3:11.

252. Matthew 4:1.

253. Luke 4:14.

254. 1 John 2:6.

255. Matthew 8:16.

256. Mark 1:25.

257. Mark 1:27.

258. The Orthodox Jewish Bible translates Leviticus 16:29 this way: *Ye shall afflict your nefashot*—to "afflict the nefesh, soul" means to fast and do physical penances in self-denial (Lv. 16:29ff.). The Jews did not separate soul and body as the Greeks did and the West has been doing.

259. Mark 9:18.

260. Mark 9:29.

261. 1 John 2:6.

262. Gedara was a region and Gerasa was a town, and all the people are correctly named Gedarenes.

263. Mark 5:8.

264. Luke 28:29.

265. Matthew 8:28 makes it two men.

266. Luke 8:37.

267. Mark 5:17.

268. Matthew 9:1.

269. Luke 8:39.

270. Luke 4:18.

271. John 9:30.

272. John 11:3. Other citations are from this passage.

273. John 10:33.

274. John 5:21.

275. John 11:7.

276. John 11:16.

277. John 12:10.

278. John 11:50.

279. Acts 2:46.

280. Mark 11:17.

281. John 7:1.

282. John 7:10.

283. John 8:2. All following citations, unless noted, are here.

284. Deuteronomy 22:22.

285. Hosea 14:4.

286. Matthew 5:20.

287. Matthew 23:6.

288. Mark 10:51.

289. Mark 1:15.

290. John 10:38.

291. John 5:4. All following citations, unless noted, are here.

292. John 5:33.

293. John 5:17, NJB.

294. Leviticus 24:16.

295. Matthew 12:14.

296. John 5:18.

297. Matthew 11:27.

298. Wisdom 7:26.

299. Colossians 1:15.

300. Malachi 4:5.

301. Deuteronomy 18:15.

302. Luke 9:31.

303. John 13:31.

304. Genesis 3:5.

305. Psalm 51:5.

306. John 15:10.

307. Matthew 26:39.

308. John 11:50.

309. Isaiah 49:6.

310. Acts 1:3.

311. Luke 9:33.

312. Romans 8:29.

313. Genesis 17:13.

314. Matthew 22:32.

315. Isaiah 42:6.

316. John 13:15.

317. John 15:5. As in other places, citations not otherwise noted are from this chapter.

318. John 17:21.

319. John 13:34.

320. John 17:6.

321. John 15:8.

322. Matthew 28:20.

323. John 6:56.

324. 1 Corinthians 11:23.

325. Pope Francis, *Laudato Si'*. All citations in this paragraph are in para. 236.

326. Ephesians 2:10.

327. *Gaudium et Spes, The Church in the Modern World,* para. 40.

328. Except for one or other very early medieval paintings, I know of only one naked Christ on His cross. It is above the entrance to a transept in the Sagrada Familia cathedral created by Gaudí in Barcelona. But it has

no face, just a square signifying his wholeness and the crown of thorns. We just can't create a complete image of so total a self-sacrifice as Jesus' was.

329. Hebrews 4:15, NJB.

330. John 11:50.

331. Isaiah 53:5.

332. John 18:21.

333. Leviticus 4:34.

334. Matthew 27:25.

335. John 10:18.

336. John 18:5.

337. A crucifix is to be "on the altar or near it, [or above it] where it is clearly visible." And the reason given is the usual one: it "calls to mind for the faithful the saving Passion of the Lord," especially his grim death. *General Instruction on the Roman Missal*, §308.

338. Gerhard Lohfink, SJ, *Jesus of Nazareth*, p. 304. There's a reason for this lapse. As *the Twelve day by day they spent much time in the Temple,* (Acts 2:46) they were expecting the Son of Man to come in his glory, escorted by all the angels, and to take his seat on his throne of glory—the Parousia, right here in the Temple. Any day, soon. The People of God are still dealing with the fact that it didn't happen.

339. See Matthew 5:1 and following; 6:6; and 10:41; Luke 6:20 and following; and 6:35.

340. Luke 18:22.

341. Matthew 25:34.

342. Matthew 19:29.

343. John 3:36.

344. John 13:15.

345. John 12:23.

346. 1 John 2:6.

347. Mark 1:15.

348. Matthew 25:31.

349. 1 Corinthians 15:19.

350. Matthew 28:6.

351. Luke 24:42.

352. Ignatius of Loyola, *Spiritual Exercises*, [299]: "he appeared to the Virgin Mary. Although this is not stated in Scripture, it is included in the statement that he appeared to so many others, for Scripture supposes that we are capable of understanding, as it is written, 'Are you also without understanding?'"

353. John 20:17.

354. Matthew 28:10.

355. John 20:17.

356. John 17:20.

357. Colossians 1:24.

358. We identify with more than one community, of course. We interpret our self and choose our identity (insofar as it is liable to free choice) by which we make first and second and last in our thoughts and actions. A Knight of Columbus will think of himself first as a Catholic—a member of the People of God—and then as a Knight. A Christian Life Community member will think of herself only second as CLC and interpret her experiences through CLC as a member of the church and Christ's.

359. Galatians 3:28.

360. Luke 24:16. Unless identified otherwise, later citations are from this chapter.

361. Isaiah 53:3.

362. Psalm 22:18.

363. Micah 5:2.

364. Matthew 1:23.

365. Judges 13:7.

366. Zephaniah 2:3.

367. Wisdom 4:15.

368. Isaiah 43:4.

369. Psalm 41:9.

370. Psalm 35:11.

371. Isaiah 53:7.

372. Isaiah 53:9.

373. Luke 24:45.

374. John 20:17.

375. Acts 4:33.

376. Romans 1.6. Paul's letter was written in the mid-fifties; Matthew, probably about 60 CE.

377. 1 Peter 1:9.

378. 1 Corinthians 3:17.

379. Colossians 1:15.

380. 1 John 2:6.

381. Luke 9:11. The Gospel of Luke and its second half, the Acts of the Apostles, was written about 70 CE.

382. Luke 24:41, NJB.

383. Luke 24:43.

384. Acts 1:3.

385. Mark 16:7.

386. John 21:3.

387. Luke 22:26, NJB.

About the Author

Joseph A. Tetlow, SJ, was ordained in 1960. He has lectured, given retreats, and written extensively on Ignatian spirituality. With a doctorate in American social and intellectual history, he has been an editor of *America* magazine and formator for younger Jesuit priests. He was Assistant for Ignatian Spirituality to the Jesuit General in Rome, lecturing and giving retreats on all five continents. His *Choosing Christ in the World* (1987) was the earliest guide for making the Exercises in Daily Life and, now in several languages, continues in use. Of his more recent books, *Making Choices in Christ* explores the theology of the *Exercises; Finding Christ in the World* applies it through prayer to everyday life; and *Always Discerning* (named best book on spirituality by the Catholic Press Association) deals with the Ignatian experience of discernment. Fr. Tetlow continues to lecture and write. He resides at Montserrat Jesuit Retreat House in Lake Dallas, Texas.